I'M A STRANGER HERE MYSELF

DERIC LONGDEN

I'M A STRANGER HERE MYSELF

BANTAM PRESS

LONDON · NEW YORK · TORONTO · SYDNEY · AUCKLAND

TRANSWORLD PUBLISHERS LTD
61–63 Uxbridge Road, London W5 5SA

TRANSWORLD PUBLISHERS (AUSTRALIA) PTY LTD
15–25 Helles Avenue, Moorebank, NSW 2170

TRANSWORLD PUBLISHERS (NZ) LTD
3 William Pickering Drive, Albany, Auckland

Published 1994 by Bantam Press
a division of Transworld Publishers Ltd
Copyright © by Deric Longden 1994
Reprinted 1994 (twice)

A catalogue record for this book
is available from the British Library
ISBN 0593 028937

Typeset in Great Britain by
Phoenix Typesetting, Ilkley, West Yorkshire.

Printed and bound in Great Britain by
Mackays of Chatham PLC, Chatham, Kent

To Pat McLoughlin,
    from me and all the other
authors she has abridged –
but not too far.
    With love and admiration.

CHAPTER ONE

Through the second-storey window I watched Mrs Bramley down in the park as she waited for Alfred to catch up with her. Alfred was getting too old to sniff at the trees nowadays. In his time he'd sniffed at each and every tree in Greenhead Park a thousand times – there was nothing new you could teach Alfred about sniffing trees.

But these days he left that to the younger dogs and their sharper noses as he fixed his one good eye on Mrs Bramley and tried to keep within barking distance of her. They were about a quarter-way around the circuit now so it must be nearly half-past ten.

Half-past ten. That's the wonderful thing about working at home, the hours are so flexible I can tie them in knots. They don't exist in real terms. I can work late into the night, tumble into bed at four o'clock in the morning and get up long after most decent God-fearing people have had their first tea-break. Just so long as I fit a good eight hours into my permutation of the twenty-four available to me, then I can live in peace with myself. I'm a smug little devil.

Come on, concentrate. Today was the day I was going

to start work on the new book. All six kids had been to stay over Christmas, together with their wives and husbands, their boyfriends and girlfriends, their live-in lovers, a granddaughter called Grace and a very small cat called Nobby.

It had been wonderful to see them all arrive and just as wonderful to see them all go – especially Nobby. And now there was space once more, space and time to think and work.

And for the first time in my life I had no idea what the book was going to be about. I had laid my life out to dry on previous pages, all the comedy and the tragedy, and now I must try something different, something that would stretch me and make me grow.

I poured myself another coffee and Mrs Bramley's image shivered as it passed through the steam rising from my mug. Then it was wiped from view completely as the top of a ladder clumped against the window-sill and Kenny's long lank hair waved me a greasy good morning.

First he nodded and then he smiled at me – he found it easier not to attempt the two actions simultaneously. I smiled and nodded at the same time just to show off.

He opened his eyes wide and then, raising his eyebrows a couple of notches, he inclined his head slightly to the left and silently mouthed the traditional window-cleaners' greeting.

'All right?'

As I mimed the answer I introduced my generous wide grin into the exchange and coupled it with one of my famous double nods.

'Fine, thank you.'

Then we smiled at each other, grinning like idiots, for several seconds before he produced an enormous sponge from about his person and slapped it against the glass.

Down in the park Alfred had given up and was sitting in the middle of the path waiting for Mrs Bramley to come back and give him the kiss of life. He ought to be on castors at his age.

Up in my office I tried to concentrate on my mail as Kenny committed atrocities upon the window-panes, each of us pretending that the other had disappeared off the face of the earth.

It's one hell of a window. Six large panes topped by six leaded lights just slightly their junior in size. I would have got up and walked away and left him to it – Aileen would be waking any minute and be ready for a cup of tea. But I just sat there and waited for him to finish, partly because I had more mail to open but mainly because I was sitting there stark naked and I didn't want him to fall off his ladder.

From where he balanced he could see only my noble head and the few grey hairs that hid the lonely muscle on my chest and that was all I wanted him to see. So I slit open envelope after envelope, not really taking in the contents because I could see he was trying to read them upside down.

Then the door opened and Aileen sailed in.

'I'm dying for a cup of tea.'

'I'll be with you in a minute – I'm just opening the mail.'

'Oh goody – is there anything for me?'

I have to read her mail to her. At a pinch she can just about decipher a letter under her close-circuit television, but it's a long and arduous business and it's much easier if I do it.

She came over and stood beside me. She put her arm around my shoulder and now at least I had something positive to do instead of just pretending for Kenny's benefit.

He must be about the worst window-cleaner I have ever come across – it was as though the daylight was being turned down a couple of degrees as he steadily creosoted the glass. He seemed to remove the dirt with his sponge and then plaster it back on with his leather. He must have served his apprenticeship on portholes. I had to admit though, he did seem to be trying harder than usual today – he'd even had a go at one of the corners.

I read Aileen a couple of rather official letters and then opened one from Lucinda, her agent. The news was exactly what she had been waiting to hear and she gave a squeal of delight. Kenny must have heard us because he grinned even though he was making out he couldn't see us.

I put my arm around her waist and gave her a squeeze and my fingers touched bare flesh. I slipped my hand up a bit and then down a bit – still bare flesh.

I swivelled my chair round and there she was – standing by my side as naked as the day she was born, not a stitch on, and Kenny was now removing the remains of a stubborn little fly with his fingernail.

Aileen had no idea he was out there – she picked up Lucinda's letter. I got to my feet.

'Come on – let's make that cup of tea.'

'Read it to me again.'

'I'll read it in your office while you have that cup of tea.'

And we walked hand in hand, slowly, all the way across the carpet towards the door. It seemed the length of a cricket pitch and I was very conscious that we were also walking cheek by cheek and that our two bare bottoms must be waving a goodbye to him in unison.

He knocked at the door about half an hour later and two cats and a kitten pushed in past him, fanning out as they left the hallway to make sure that the dreaded Nobby had really gone.

'That'll be seven pounds fifty.'

'There's no hurry,' I told him. 'You can pay me anytime.'

To his credit he smiled, a watery sort of smile that evaporated before it had time to make an impression.

'Go on then,' he said. 'I'll knock fifty pence off for the entertainment.'

It's quite a sobering thought really. Fifty pence – for the two of us. We wouldn't make a bare living in the strip-o-gram business.

I fed the cats. Tigger had her tuna in spring water

up on the far worktop so that Thermal couldn't get at it. Thermal had his on the other side of the pedalbin so that Frink wouldn't see, and Frink had a saucer of kitten-building Whiskas down by the side of the fridge, well away from her marauding elders. By the time I had taken two strides out of the kitchen they would all have swopped round and be at different saucers. I don't know why I bother.

We have two kitchens. A long-by-narrow galley on the office floor and, below decks, a dining kitchen straight out of *Good Housekeeping*. It's beautiful and functional and it cost us an arm and a leg, two kidneys and a ruptured spleen. We eat downstairs and the cats eat up in the galley.

That is, in theory. In practice they sat in a drooling line by the dishwasher and watched me as I peeled open an individual packet of Coco-Pops. They would each of them give their right paw for a Coco-Pop.

Aileen and I wouldn't – we don't like Coco-Pops, they make your milk go brown. It's just that in every Kellog's Variety pack you get one packet of Coco-Pops. It's the price you pay for buying your breakfast cereals in handy bite-sized packets and it's a price we pay willingly. We get bored with the same old cereal day after day. They begin to take you for granted after a while and stop trying. They let themselves go, and there's nothing worse than a flabby cornflake.

The Coco-Pop population had flourished in the back of the cupboard and were becoming something of a problem. We had twenty-three tiny packets in there a week ago, but the kids had culled the herd over Christmas and now I felt honour-bound to put the sole survivor out of his misery. I closed my eyes and tried to pretend they were Honey Nut Loops.

Aileen sat opposite me and munched on her toast as she listened to Woman's Hour on the portable radio clipped to her belt. I sat opposite her and watched her earpieces rising and falling as she chewed. She swallowed and they did a little somersault – I'm sure her ears don't do that when they're on their own.

'I've had an idea,' I told her.

'Female circumcision,' she said.

'No.'

She reached out hesitantly, trying to locate her cup. She found it but couldn't find the handle – it was round the other side of the cup, it always is.

'An idea about the book.'

'Jenni's talking to a Somali woman.'

'Right.'

'She's been circumcised.'

I think she meant the Somali woman. I'd like to see somebody try and circumcise Jenni Murray – she'd have them for breakfast. I tried again.

'You know Peter Mayle's *A Year In Provence?*'

'It's horrible . . .'

'Yes I know, but it's sold well.'

'. . . they cut off the lips of the vagina.'

'I'm going to write a parody. I'm going to call it *A Year In Huddersfield*.'

I waited for her reaction. She was searching for her cigarettes now. She found mine and lit one.

'What do you think?'

'It happens in this country as well.'

'My point exactly. I think I'll have a go at it.'

It was good to get her blessing. We work independently but we value each other's opinion.

That afternoon I settled down to work on the first chapter. I don't know how Kingsley Amis sets about writing, but I always begin by clearing out the cellar. Before I had a cellar I would clean the cooker – perhaps that's what Kingsley does.

I work on the principle that, since I never concentrate on what I am supposed to be doing, I am far better off tackling some mundane task than just sitting there staring at my Amstrad for hours on end. My mind can then float off on its own as I drop stiff paint-brushes into a dustbin liner and sort out the screws from the nails.

Arthur sat on the central-heating boiler and watched gloomily as I tidied up around him. I am very fond of Arthur. He's a throwback from the old flat-cap days – a cat of very few words, and he was using two of them now.

'Bugger off.'

He arrived a year ago – a mangy old stray with two broken back legs and a tail to match. Now, thanks to a balanced diet and a vet's bill as long as your arm, his coat always looks as though it has just come back from Sketchleys and even if his rear legs still aren't talking to one another, they are strong enough for him to get about – just as long as he doesn't want to go in a straight line.

'It won't take long, Arthur – just sorting things out.'

The cellar belongs to Arthur and he doesn't like change of any sort. If he needs to pop out for anything he has his private cat-flap at the foot of the old basement steps, but his needs are few and he spends most of his days contemplating the meaning of life and warming his bum on the boiler.

We have given up trying to entice him upstairs to be with the other cats. He'll nod to them as they pass in the courtyard and even stop for a chat if he comes across one of them out for a stroll on a warm summer's evening, but he's not one for crowds and he prefers to be down in the cellar with his own things around him and his memories of what it was like in the old days.

As I cleared around him I began to chew on my idea. We had more characters per square yard in Huddersfield than Provence could throw up in a month of Sundays, and like Peter Mayle we were trying to put an old house back together again. Outside, high on the wall, the original owners had had their initials carved on a stone plaque – a flowery WHM. Now, a hundred years later, we were determined that if ever William and Harriet Murgatroyd happened to be passing by and looked in on us, they would smile fondly and give us their blessing. The house would be much as they remembered it.

I remembered my first sight of Huddersfield – a place I had always associated with Hell, Hull and Halifax. It was dusk and it was raining, a thin drizzle stirring the flies into a thick syrup on my windscreen. There was a petrol station – I was short of petrol . . . that was it, that was my opening. I dropped the bin liner on the floor with a thump and turned to address the boiler.

'I'm going upstairs, Arthur.'

'*Don't let me stop you.*'

'I've had an idea.'

'*There's a first time for everything.*'

JANUARY

I wasn't going to make it. Through a curtain of white rain I could see the street lights of Huddersfield as they held hands down in the valley. On the dashboard a cocky little amber light told me I had about half a pint of petrol left in the tank.

It had been on at me ever since I left the motorway – they panic easily, these amber lights. I ignored it. I had no option – my wallet was in my leather jacket and my leather jacket was hanging on a peg seventy-five miles away.

I switched off the engine and coasted and the lights went out and the wipers stopped and the brakes didn't work. I switched it back on and the little amber light came to life once more and smirked at me. I hit it – but it took no notice.

As I rounded the next bend I saw the petrol station. I assumed it was a petrol station – it had a pump. The Luddites had missed this one. The amber light must have seen it at the same time because it went all miserable and the engine coughed and died as we coasted to a halt by a sign that read 'No Diesel'.

I didn't want any diesel. I checked the change in my pocket. I wanted ninety-seven pence worth of petrol.

There was a man in a hut reading *Dalton's Weekly*. He looked up as I pushed open the door.

'Excuse me – do you think I could have ninety-seven pence worth of petrol?'

'It all depends.'

'On what?'

'If you've got ninety-seven pence.'

'That's all I have got.'

'Then there's no problem.'

He put the paper aside and led the way. There was no question of self-service here – it would have taken him a fortnight to teach me how to use the pump.

He cranked it up and drip fed the petrol, penny by penny, into the tank. With a modern pump it would have taken all of two seconds. Here I got my money's worth.

'How far are you going?'

'Just into town.'

'Oh you'll make it all right.'

I gave him the money and he began to count the coins, slowly, as he leaned against the door.

'Thank you very much.'

He nodded. 'My pleasure.'

The engine spluttered into life and the little amber light bounced back into action – but then, as the truth sank in, all the fire went out of it and it just sat there in the dashboard and sulked.

I yanked the seat-belt over my shoulder and slipped off the handbrake. The man rattled the coins in his hand.

'What exactly are you trying to do – wean it?'

I eased the car back on to the narrow road and my headlights picked out a fading signpost as it relaxed against an old stone wall. It read, 'Huddersfield – 5 miles.'

I had a feeling I was going to like it here.

And yet as a child I had known this county only as the home of my natural enemy. I spent days watching cricket in the Queen's Park Chesterfield as Derbyshire did battle with Yorkshire. Even though it was barely twelve miles away Yorkshire was very much a foreign country to me, and once a year the invaders would come storming over the border to steal our women, rape our sheep and beat us by an innings and twenty-five runs.

Their heads were as big as their backsides and they were insufferable as they pounded their way to victory year after year. Whether they would have been as modest in defeat I never found out.

A man selling the *Sheffield Star* from an enormous red bag slung over his shoulder would carve his way around the boundary and rub salt into the wound.

'Tykes topple Derbyshire – read all about it.'

Ten yards behind him an older man tottered with a much smaller bag – a *Derby Evening Telegraph* jacket over his shabby raincoat.

'Get your *Telegraph* – nothing good ever came out of Yorkshire.'

The memory of those huge white-flannelled backsides had stayed with me ever since. Powerful, intimidating and supremely confident, they ran roughshod over the Pennines. The female variety hoisted high in the Sheffield air as their owners scrubbed the front doorstep – the more muscular male counterpart, like an enormous outboard motor, driving a pair of taut trousers along the pavement and defying you to pass.

There were two of them in front of me the next morning, two Yorkshiremen barring my way, as I took my first few tentative steps through the streets of Huddersfield. At first glance it could have been Freddie Trueman and Geoffrey Boycott striding along John William Street, except that they were holding hands.

I followed as they carried along New Street, fascinated, my eyes on the intertwining fingers as they played games with one another – the thumbs gently playing a less obvious game of their own.

The two figures stopped at the corner of Cloth Hall Street and then the pair of brown no-nonsense trousers turned and planted themselves in front of the light blue cords.

'Now I want you home for your tea.'

'I will be.'

'Five-thirty – no later.'

'I'll be there.'

I had stopped now and was half-heartedly examining the Midland Bank cash dispenser, fine-tuning my ears so that they reached the edge of the pavement.

'I'm not wasting my time cooking for it to be spoilt.'

'Don't worry.'

'You said that last night.'

'I'm sorry about last night.'

'Ah well – just so it doesn't happen again.'

'It won't.'

And with that they kissed each other lightly on the cheek and after a nice long hug for good measure they each went their separate way, one perhaps to his iron foundry and the other to his lathe.

A woman touched me on the shoulder.

'You have to put your card in, you know – it's not a mind reader.'

I left her tapping in her pin number and braced myself against the New Street gale that hurls itself straight off the moors and then pipes itself along the urban canyon, pausing only to pop in at the Co-op on the way.

I had never considered the possibility of there being any such animal as a gay Yorkshireman. It had never figured in my calculations.

I slipped in behind a mobile windbreak who, with her two large shopping bags and three small children, didn't even seem to notice there was so much as a breath of wind about the place. I pulled my coat collar up around my ears. It seemed there was a lot I had to learn about Huddersfield.

I sat back and read it through a final time. Well, it was a start – probably wouldn't finish up anything like that, but it was a start.

Thermal, who had spent the afternoon sunbathing under my anglepoise lamp, gave a polite cough.

'What is it?'

He nodded towards the door and I turned to see Aileen staring at me. She can never tell whether I'm lost in concentration or fast asleep. Either way she waits for me to say something before interrupting – she's very thoughtful.

She had a computer disc in her hand. Over the years she has evolved a very clever method of telling which disc is which. Since she can't print titles on the labels large enough for her to read, she has had the discs colour-coded; red for the book she's working on at present, blue for her previous book, green for accounts – that sort of thing. That way she can pick out the disc she needs at a glance. It's a very clever system.

'Yes, love?'

'What colour is that?'

'It's a blue one.'

'Thank you.'

Of course it isn't a perfect system, but it looked good on paper.

CHAPTER TWO

That nice Mr Kettley had said it was going to snow today and I was rather looking forward to it. We had the odd flake or two yesterday and it had taken me by surprise – that small Scotsman who also does the weather on the BBC might have mentioned it but I can never tell what he says, he sort of loses me as soon as he takes his first breath. He uses free-range commas and they tend to stray somewhat.

We had snow when I lived in Matlock and we were very proud of it. It was an annual event and the snow was of the deep and crisp and even variety that stuck to the hillsides and drifted over walls, blocking the highways and byways. We had a sign declaring Matlock to be, 'The Switzerland of England'.

As soon as the roads became impassable, the entire population would reverse out of their garages and head for Crown Square, where they immediately got stuck up to their back axles. They would then abandon the car and head for the nearest pub and a large whisky, claiming that it was for medicinal purposes you see.

Midlands Television would tell us that night of wide-spread chaos in the area and show us a scrawny shot of a

Ford Cortina struggling to cope with a half an inch of mucky slush on the outskirts of Birmingham. We would boo loudly, hoot with derision and then order another large whisky.

And so I was looking forward to the snow here in Huddersfield – it promised to be quite something. So far it had only been of the pansy variety, the timid sort of stuff that doesn't want to be too much of a nuisance.

But I wasn't to be fooled. Out there on the ring road, just before you turn up into Trinity Street and head out towards the M62, was a sign that read, 'When this light is flashing the road is blocked with snow.' And this was a permanent sign that stood high and proud – not some pathetic little triangular tin thing held down by a couple of sandbags to stop it blowing away. It was there all the year round – even in August.

I just couldn't wait to do battle with this *samurai* snow and only hoped that my earlier training in the hills of Derbyshire had fitted me to cope.

But when I parted the curtains that morning the flagstones in the courtyard were still there for all the world to see, merely fringed by a little light frost that had summoned up just about enough energy to give them a tickle. Never mind – we still had February to come and I remembered Buxton on a day in June when snow had brought the county cricket to a halt. Mustn't lose heart – maybe up here in Huddersfield it wouldn't reach its peak until August.

There was a great mewing from the cat's kitchen and Thermal marched out to tell me that there were cats dying of starvation in there.

'*And you know the trouble Arthur has with his blood sugar.*'

I knew only too well – he had told me often enough. If he didn't have a square meal every hour, on the hour, he would pass out and not have the strength to eat the next one. It was a vicious circle, he said.

They were lined up facing the cooker, shortest on the left, tallest on the right. They always seemed to think that if they stared hard enough at the oven door it would miraculously fly open to reveal a ready-cooked chicken with all the trimmings.

I plucked a couple of tins from the cupboard behind them and there was a collective sigh as they wheeled round like the Tiller girls for yet another cold collation.

The cooker had been giving us problems. It was enormous, and it lurked at the far end of the kitchen like a small bus pulled up at a request stop. Every time I came in I felt I ought to make a run for it before the conductor dinged his bell and it swung out into the traffic.

We had inherited it along with the house. It was long and white with two great big ovens and a warming drawer in which you could have serviced a Ford Escort. It had a separate grill and electric rings at frequent intervals along its length, with acres of white space in between.

The switches, knobs and dials were set in a long white panel edged in Buick chrome like some Mission Control from an early American film. I never knew which switch to flick or knob to turn. Captain Kirk would have been able to tell me, it was right up his street.

We hardly ever used it, we had the new one with its ceramic hob downstairs, but it seemed a shame to let it just lie there, falling into disrepute, and so Aileen had talked to a friend who knew a man who knew about these things.

'He's weird,' they said, 'but he does know about cookers.'

If he was weird he would feel at home with our cooker. I leaned over and tried the knob on the left and a dial twitched. I tried its next door neighbour and my groin lit up as the grill burst into life.

I wanted that ring over there, the one in the distance with the small white kitten sitting on it. Better get her off first and then try. She grumbled but I'm bigger than she is and she sat on the draining board and watched me, her tail dripping down into a milk pan that had been soaking overnight.

'What are you doing?' Aileen wanted to know as she drifted in behind me.

'Finding out what's wrong with it.'

'Everything's wrong with it.'

'I know.'

'Tell him that then.'

She has a way of getting down to basics that has always eluded me.

He wasn't on the phone, which was why we were looking for an old weaver's cottage on the edge of nowhere, a nowhere that was becoming more and more treacherous with black ice. Actually it looked like brown ice to me but maybe that was because I was wearing my tinted sunglasses to cut down on the glare.

'It must be around here somewhere.'

'Don't worry – we'll find it eventually.'

Aileen is always remarkably tolerant of my inability to find my way about. Perhaps it's because she can't help me and she only likes to compete on equal terms.

'Try down there.'

I turned down the lane I had ignored a couple of times already, the lane where the cottage couldn't possibly be, and there they were, four of them all in a row.

'Could it be one of those?'

'Could be.'

'I wonder which one?'

Privately I plumped for the cottage with the skeletal remains of a cooker standing in the front garden, the one with the grillpan on the front doorstep.

'That one, I think.'

'Right – let's have a go then.'

The cookerman's wife answered the door and led us through to a small sitting-room, whereupon Aileen immediately trod on a small dog. It was a weedy, rather bewildered-looking pug and it was his fault, he tried to sniff Aileen's knees and she doesn't see small dogs. We apologized and I stroked him, trying to smooth down his fur to cover the marks from Aileen's high heels, as she told our story to the cookerman's wife.

'Sit down.'

We sat down. I sat on a settee, the wife sat in a winged easy and Aileen sat on the dog – it seemed a rather unfortunate little dog and I apologized to him once more as I pulled him out from underneath.

'Come here, Lucky,' said the cookerman's wife and he limped over to join her.

'He'll only do it if he feels like it,' she went on and we both stared at the dog. Perhaps it was a kamikaze pug that enjoyed hurling its tiny body under the feet and bottoms of human beings. Then we realized that she was talking about her husband when she added, 'He's down in the shed at the moment.'

For the next fifteen minutes or so we were sub-jected to an acid monologue that had the two of us and the dog riveted to the spot.

'Only the other night I turned round to him and I said Cyril, I said, you can't go on being so choosy – then he turned round to me and said I'll be as choosy as I like – so I turned round to him and I said everyone's money is as good as everyone else's – and he turned round to me and he said it's my life – so I turned round to him and said it's my life as well – well, he turned round to me and he said . . .'

I had this image of two people who spent their entire lives with their backs to one another, turning round only to hurl the odd phrase in the general direction of the other.

Then Cyril walked in and my heart did a somersault as I realized that chapter two of my new book had just entered my life under its own steam.

I could see why she should want to spend her life with her back to him – he was the spitting image of Jack Nicholson all dressed up for *The Shining*. He had long black hair and fingernails to match and his face suggested it was early closing day.

He walked over and switched on the television, then sat down. I apologized for dropping in unannounced like this.

'Only you're not on the phone.'

'If you have a phone,' he muttered, 'people keep ringing you up.'

I couldn't argue with that and, fielding Aileen's 'Are we wise to place our cooker's life in this man's hands?' look, I ploughed on and mentioned the name of the friend who had recommended him.

He never took his eyes off the television.

'She's a Neff,' he said. 'Are you a Neff?'

I didn't know whether I was a neff or not, but Aileen came to the rescue.

'Westinghouse,' she told him. 'Westinghouse Cavalcade.'

The very mention of the name had a remarkable effect on him. He snapped off the television with a remote control that he somehow furked out from underneath the dog and then stood up.

'I'm going out, Muriel – I could be some time.'

For a moment I thought I was witnessing a re-run of *Scott of the Antarctic*.

'Come on,' he ordered and then strode out of the front door.

He drove behind us all the way home in his van and yet he was already stamping impatiently on the front doorstep while I was still locking the garage. Out in the open air he looked even more like Jack Nicholson.

'Go and open the door for him, Aileen, before he sets about it with an axe.'

He didn't just examine the cooker – he made love to it, running his hands all over its vitreous enamel body, stroking its rounded curves and caressing its important little places.

'I've only ever seen one of these before – it was in Canada,' he breathed. 'You're beautiful, aren't you?'

The cooker didn't answer in so many words – it just simpered and then fluttered its extractor hood at him. We left the two of them alone together. It was embarrassing – as though we were intruding.

About an hour later he emerged and told us the worst. It needed this and it needed that, lots of technical bits and pieces that you couldn't get in this country.

'I can make 'em though – cost you £348.'

We jibbed at that. We thought we might as well buy a new cooker, something more compact. His look was one of pure disgust.

'A new one? They only make rubbish these days – you've got a Rolls-Royce and you want to buy a Reliant Robin? Cost you thousands new, this would.'

Well, we rather liked the idea of having a Rolls-Royce, even if it was only a cooker. I was already thinking in terms of a personalized number plate – DL1 would look rather well.

And so we told him to go ahead and he went back into the kitchen to break the good news. His voice was so gentle as he reassured the cooker, Muriel wouldn't have recognized him.

'Don't you worry, my love, we'll soon have you right.'

He stayed another quarter of an hour or so, measuring up and making notes and then after he had left we slipped into the kitchen ourselves to take a fresh look at our new status-symbol.

It seemed happier somehow, now it had found someone who understood. He had wiped it over with a damp cloth and the wet hot-plate gleamed an unnatural black against the white enamel.

A greasy handprint spread itself on the control panel, the fingertips teasing the manual knob.

'You ought to be ashamed of yourself,' I told the cooker, as I wiped it away with a length of kitchen towel.

I went straight into the office and began making notes about the cookerman and his wife, squeezing myself with pleasure as I jotted down their lines. I have perfect pitch for dialogue as long as I don't allow eight hours' sleep to intervene.

Two of the cats, Thermal and Tigger, were sitting on the window-ledge pulling faces at passers-by, but they raced over to tell me as soon as it started to snow. It wasn't much, just a few flakes, but Thermal gets very excited. He'd been on at me for ages to buy him a sledge, but it hardly seems worth it just for a few days a year, does it?

Anyway, I eased open the back door so they could have a proper look and, long before the gap was wide enough for a cat only half his size, Thermal was through it and out on to the balcony.

He raced towards the steps and Tigger was giving me a look as though to say 'Men!' when all of a sudden Thermal hit a patch of black ice. He was all over the place – he hadn't changed to winter paws, he didn't have enough tread, and he shot sideways out of control, crashed down the first three steps, banged into the railings, skidded down the other steps and came to rest on his bottom on the first landing.

Well, I tried not to laugh, but Tigger gave me a great big grin and it set me off. Then she very carefully and gingerly picked her way down the steps so that she could grin at him from close quarters; by the time she had made it he had already picked himself up and limped away to lick his wounds in private.

'Did he hurt himself?' asked Aileen when I told her.

'No – you know what he's like, he bounces.'

'He'll bounce once too often,' she said.

It must have been half an hour or so later before I went to let them back in. It can be an unnerving experience. You have to whip the door open quickly and stand back, because as soon as he hears you coming along the hall Thermal starts running, and by the time you've flicked the latch he has already hit thirty miles an hour and he comes through the doorway like an express train and doesn't stop until he hits the hall mirror.

So I wrenched open the door and stood back – nothing. Then Tigger tripped in, daintily, as though she were on a tightrope, to be followed after a decent interval by a small war veteran who had been to hell and back.

I thought about taking him straight round to the vet, but I know what he's like – he puts it on, so I made a big fuss of him and he loved that. I offered him a slice from yesterday's roast but he was far too ill to eat it.

He went through his repertoire of death scenes from the movies instead, starting with Marlon Brando in *The Godfather*. It's a somewhat limited repertoire, but he plays them for all they are worth. He was just winding up for his *Tale of Two Cities* when I decided it would be a far, far better thing if I left him to it and went and did some work.

The limp was real enough though. I could see him now through the crack in the door as he hobbled into the kitchen to see if I had left the security alarm off the roast beef. It's no fun playing death scenes to an empty house.

My mother would have known what to do. I missed my conversations with my mother – she always had a solution on the tip of her tongue.

'*You know what's wrong with him, don't you? – it's probably psychosomatic.*'

She would have heard that on BBC2 some months back and have been saving it up, just for an occasion such as this.

'*It happened to some soldiers who were gassed in World War One.*'

That bit might have come from a programme on Radio 4 that she heard by mistake as she twiddled the knob.

'He's just pulled a muscle – he slipped on the ice.'

She wouldn't have believed that there wasn't more to it than that, but she would have humoured me. If I hadn't the intellectual equipment to handle the deeper issues in life then there was little else she could do.

'*Have you tried Savlon? – I find it works wonders.*'

That brought back memories. Poor old Whisky. If her long-suffering old cat embarked on the most perfunctory of scratches she wouldn't reach for the flea powder – she would plaster him all over with Savlon.

'*It works,*' she used to say.

It worked because it took him so long to lick off the ointment that he forgot all about the fleas for at least a fortnight. I shall never forget the look of absolute distaste on his sad little face as he plunged his tongue deep into the greasy fur.

I think it took the fleas by surprise as well. One minute they were having a good old bite – showing the kids how it should be done – the next they were up to their eyeballs in an oil slick and wondering where the nearest PDSA was.

Whisky would never have known how many aspirins were broken up and mixed with his Tunafish Surprise. She gave him sleeping tablets, blood and stomach pills, and once he had a course of Zantac when she thought he had an ulcer.

I remember her dosing his KiteKat with a laxative that had been prescribed for my Aunty Jessie. The results were spectacular – I don't think he sat still for a month.

Thermal didn't know how lucky he was to have an enlightened owner like me. I'd give him a day or so and if his leg wasn't better by then I would take him to the vet. Failing that there was always the Savlon.

Four days later I had a telephone call from the cookerman's wife. He would be coming round at ten o'clock the next morning.

'He's hardly been to bed these past few days. Been in his workshop all the time. I keep telling him he'll have a breakdown but he won't listen. I told him when I took him a cup of tea down this morning, I said – you think more of your cookers than you do of me and he turned round to me and he said . . .'

Mercifully her money ran out at that point and so I never heard what he turned round and said to her, but

I did hear him whispering to the cooker the next day as I listened at the kitchen door.

'Now then, old girl, doesn't that feel better? You just wait until I've fitted your new thermostat – then you'll notice the difference.'

He sounded almost human, but he reverted to type the moment I pushed open the door to ask him if he wanted a cup of coffee.

He had dragged the cooker out into the middle of the floor and they both started with surprise and looked up guiltily as I entered.

Then it was my turn to look shamefaced. It's not the sort of cooker you pull out all that often. It weighs a ton, and behind where it had once stood a five-foot long mattress of fluff was attempting to climb the kitchen wall.

'I wondered where that had gone,' I mumbled, plucking a plastic spatula from the woolly pile. How an entire regiment of raisins had got down there was a mystery. Either they had taken a wrong turn on a route march or one of the cats had posted them down the back of the cooker. Of course they might not be raisins at all – we could have a wild rabbit loose in the kitchen.

Cyril gave me a look that suggested he was about to report me to the authorities for criminal neglect whilst in charge of a cooker, so I quickly made the coffee and left them to it.

Six hours later he had finished and the cooker looked as though it had just stepped out of a dream sequence. He had brillo-padded it and oven-padded it, buffed it and polished it – he might even have starched it – until it shone like a beacon against the kitchen wall. He had done everything except give it a centre parting.

The fluff had been captured and trapped in a bucket, the floor had been scrubbed to provide the perfect setting and the surrounding tiles now formed a sterile halo around the control panel.

'I think it's wonderful . . .' I began, but he wasn't on my wavelength. He was in another world altogether, down on his knees taking Polaroid snaps from this angle and from that angle. Any minute he would ask the cooker to say cheese.

Patrick, my next door neighbour, walked in and he was so impressed that it was almost a pleasure to part with the money. Cyril counted the notes quickly, with his back to the cooker so that their relationship wouldn't be sullied by the commercial side of the deal.

I opened the oven door, half expecting a blast of heavenly music to issue forth, and Patrick knelt and touched the shining shelves.

'You've done one hell of a job,' he said. 'Would you come and have a look at mine?'

'What sort is it?' Cyril asked over his shoulder and Patrick had to think for a moment.

'It's a Tricity,' he said.

Cyril turned, snorted in disgust and, without another word, marched straight out of my life for ever.

Aileen was just as impressed as Patrick had been.

'I think you should use it tonight,' she said. 'Let's have a celebratory dinner.'

'All right. What do you fancy?'

'Beans on toast'll do.'

'Beans on toast it is then.'

I opened a tin and bundled them into a pan, then slipped a couple of slices of bread under the grill. The cooker shook its head and sighed.

'You ought to be ashamed of yourself,' it said.

CHAPTER THREE

The barbarian hordes have raped John William Street. Ronald McDonald should be hanged, drawn and quarter-pounded for what he's done to his corner of what was once an elegant thoroughfare.

And yet if you walk along its length with an arm slightly raised to block out the street-level sabotage inflicted by the monstrous regiment of retailers, you can still see, in the stones that rise above, the dreams of the men who built it.

They had class, those builders. The railway station is magnificent as long as you don't try to go inside it and the Town Hall is magnificent even if you do. With Jane Glover and The Huddersfield Choral Society up on the stage, then it's the eighth, ninth and tenth wonders of the world all rolled into one.

I am sure those proud builders would like me to say categorically, here and now, that they had nothing whatsoever to do with the building of Currys electrical emporium on the edge of town. They didn't build aircraft hangars in their day, there was no call for them.

To be accurate it's really a semi-detached aircraft hangar.

MFI have the other half. Perhaps MFI built it – maybe it came in a box. Maybe it *is* the box.

Still, it was very handy when Aileen decided to come out of hibernation for a few brief moments. We were able to taxi right up to the front door and slip into the warehouse without February even noticing she'd ever left the house. She refuses to have anything to do with February – she's had enough of winter by then, she says.

She wanted to buy a television with a screen large enough for her to be able to see Gordon the Gopher without having to climb inside the set.

She sits on the floor at home, right up close, her nose poking in amongst the static. But no matter how close she gets, she has yet to catch even the merest glimpse of Gordon and it cuts her out of the conversation at the more sophisticated dinner parties.

The young man in the smart suit tracked us across the floor until he had us cornered by a television screen the size of an early Odeon cinema.

'If you need any help . . .'

'Is this the largest you have?'

'Yes.'

'We'll take it.'

He wasn't used to making a sale as easily as that and he tried to justify his existence by explaining what all the buttons were for. Mrs Singh of Sundal Corner would have envied him – she always has to deal with Aileen's outrageous demands for more and more discount until the only solution would seem to be arm-wrestling.

But February is no month for haggling. This is the ragged end of winter, and her enthusiasm for horsetrading goes underground until the spring sunshine appears and the sap begins to rise once more.

'Will you be able to get it in the car?'

We would have more chance of getting the car into the television set, so they agreed to deliver it. Three strong men and a fork-lift truck would have little trouble easing it up to the lounge on the second floor.

As we left the car park I caught sight of the MFI logo in the rear-view mirror. I have happy memories of MFI. My mother's favourite place for a day out was Chatsworth Park and then Van Dyke's nursery, with MFI running it close in third place. She was a strange woman, but it didn't do anyone any harm and it was a cheap enough way to spend an afternoon.

'*Let's go and have a look at MI5.*'

'*All right.*'

She would spend some time examining a sideboard-cum-display cabinet, running her hands over the glass doors and shelves. Then she would bend down and try to ease one end up off the floor.

'*I wonder how they get all that in a box?*'

'*Beats me.*'

'*Amazing, isn't it.*'

Then we would move on to stand and stare at a complete bedroom laid out in an alcove and wonder how they got all that in a box.

'*I suppose the duvet will come separately.*'

'*I should imagine so.*'

She had tremendous respect for MFI's ingenuity. She never bought anything but she certainly got her money's worth.

My stomach rumbled and brought me back to the present day. Aileen hadn't even noticed that I had been away.

'Why don't we go for a pub lunch?' I suggested.

To my surprise she agreed. She loves nothing better than a Yorkshire pudding in onion gravy – it brings out the flavour of the gin and tonic, she says – but this was February and she had given up on living until March.

'What about the Albert?' she said.

The old corner pub hummed with life – I sometimes think the town is run from the Albert. The Council rubber-stamp the decisions in the Town Hall, but it's in the Albert, just across the street, round the corner and down a bit, that those decisions are thrashed out and brought to life.

We eased our way through to a far corner table. The old man on the end was dismissing politics with a wave of his hand.

'I've given up voting myself – it only encourages 'em.'

I wish I could write lines like that. Still, beggars can't be choosers, and at least I was the only one in the pub with sense enough to pull out a notepad and jot it down under cover of the table.

He might be able to answer my question. Yesterday morning I had driven through Derby and seen the sign 'Twinned with Osnabruck' mounted on the grass verge.

'Do you happen to know if Huddersfield is twinned with anywhere?'

'I've no idea,' he told me, 'but we do have a suicide-pact with Otley.'

Chapter two of my embryo book hove into view as I flipped open the notepad on my knee once more. And as Aileen chatted up the old man and a malt whisky mysteriously appeared in front of me, the conversation disappeared into the far distance and I began to put it together in my head.

FEBRUARY

I can't be bothered with pubs in the summer – I have no interest in sitting at a table on the lawn outside, coping with small children and other insects. I like to have battled my way through pouring rain or drifting snow towards that welcoming red table lamp in the window. I can keep February at arm's length as I stamp my feet in front of a roaring log fire and turn the large malt whisky in my hand, waiting for that golden moment as it slides right down and touches my toes.

Perhaps it's the everlasting influence of those old romantic Christmas cards with a coach and four horses pulled up outside and the bright red faces of the passengers who are on their way in. Perhaps it's an unconscious desire to revisit the womb – I don't know what it is. Somehow these places don't have the same appeal in the summer.

There is no shortage of roaring log fires in and around Huddersfield and the raw material for a writer is to be found playing darts or dominoes or staring absently into a pint glass.

The wisps of conversation, drawn by the draught from the chimney, float slowly past my ear, just waiting to be caught.

'Have they got any children?'

'No. They can't have any – and he'd just had an extension built on.'

There are some pubs that cater for the chattering classes, and you'll find the odd teenage crèche here and there with its blasting disco and its designer beers.

But the proper pubs in Yorkshire have an added ingredient that you'll be hard put to find in other pubs around the country – they're usually chock-full of Yorkshiremen. Silence is golden and the small talk is kept to the minimum.

I have a theory that if a Yorkshireman decides to pay you a compliment he first has to go to a small government office just outside Cleckheaton where they will issue him with a ration book. It's a bit of a bind all that bureaucracy, which explains why he will invariably have just the one coupon left and not be too anxious to waste it.

And so the other night, when the lady who had been sipping a gin and tonic at my elbow for the past half hour suddenly cleared her throat, everyone in the pub seemed to sense that something remarkable was about to happen.

'I just wanted to say that I've read your wife's books and I saw her on television the other night and I thought she looked lovely and what with her handicap – well, I think she's marvellous.'

And with that she was gone. It was enough of an ordeal having to pay the compliment without suffering the agony of receiving my stumbling thanks.

If it hadn't been for her accent the assembled audience would merely have assumed that she must have come from down south and didn't know any better – thank God it didn't happen all that often.

And they would have relaxed and settled down to some serious drinking, if it hadn't been for the unnerving realization that the Typical Yorkshireman at the far end of the bar was about to add his twopennorth to this astonishing outburst.

He didn't have a flat cap and he didn't have a whippet, but he did have a pint in his hand and he was inching sideways towards me from the other end of the bar.

Worse still – he was going to say something. He didn't quite know what it was yet, but he was going to say something.

He never once took his eyes from the ceiling as he came nearer and nearer, crablike down the bar, until his shoulder was touching mine.

'I couldn't help overhearing – what is it that's wrong with your wife?'

'She's blind.'

He took a sip from his glass.

'Is she deaf?'

'No – she's not deaf.'

He took another sip.

'Ah well – it's summat, in't it.'

And with that he sidled back to his place, sliding his glass along in front of him, eyes still up there on the low beams.

I was so touched. The exchange had taken more out of him than a whole bucketful of tears from Bob Monkhouse and he was now explaining his behaviour to his embarrassed friends.

'Well – it needed saying.'

We drove home by the ring road. The snow-warning light was still off duty and sulking up there on its pole, unlike its younger brother on my dashboard who was once again telling me in no uncertain terms that I had but a few pints of fuel left in the tank.

'I need some petrol,' I told Aileen.

'Oh – myee love . . .' she sang sweetly along with the bald gentleman from the pop group Right Said Fred.

'It won't take a minute.'

'. . . let's set sail on seas of passion.'

'Yes all right – just let me get some petrol first.'

There are those who, when taking petrol at a filling station, try to get exactly ten pounds' worth. There are those who stop when the nozzle cuts out, and then there are those who still go on taking petrol in ever decreasing amounts until it spills over and ruins their brand new Hush Puppies. I'm one of those – I should really wear wellingtons and an oilskin when I'm filling up at a petrol station.

I slipped the nozzle back into its socket and reached in my pocket for my car keys. My car is a Lancia and I think the Italians must have smaller hands than we brawny British. There's no way I can get my fingers round the filler cap to screw it back on, there isn't enough space in the recess and I have to whizz it round with my ignition key.

I'm quite good at it now. It's just a matter of practice – a quick twist of the wrist to set the filler cap spinning, then I keep it going with the key, just like a whip and top, while it threads itself back into position.

I gave it a quick flick and the cap shot straight up in the air and the keys shot straight down the petrol tank, like a rabbit making for home.

Now I could have panicked – I'm quite good at that, I've had a lot of practice. But I didn't, I just stood there and looked bewildered – I'm *very* good at that.

A bewildered look can be very handy at times. In supermarkets ladies come up to you and ask if you are all right.

'I can't find the pickled walnuts.'

'Come with me love, I'll show you.'

On the forecourt of the petrol station I could have

37

stood there and looked bewildered for a fortnight and a fat lot of good it would have done me. Aileen was lost to the world as she sat on the dock of the bay alongside Otis Reading, helping him out with vocal refrain and accompanying him on dashboard and gearstick.

I seem to have been blessed with women who find it impossible not to join in the moment they hear an opening chord. My mother's favourite was,

'A you're so beautiful,
B you're so wonderful,
C you're the starlight in my eyes.'

The words changed every time she had a go at it, but I never once heard her get in touch with the alphabet. I don't think she understood the point of it all.

I stood there by the petrol pump awaiting the tidal wave of self-recrimination to flood over me; waiting to hear my father's voice.

'I don't know – what are we going to do with you?'

He's never around when I have a book published or save the cat from drowning, but just let me drop my keys in a fuel tank or spill petrol over my shoes and he's the first one on the scene.

'It was your own fault.'
'I know it was.'
'You'll never learn.'

He was even worse before he died.

And then a rather pleasant feeling swept over me, the wonderful realization that I had prepared for this moment some time ago. About a year earlier I had Sellotaped a spare key to the front nearside hub-cap.

The weak-kneed wimp who always wants to curl up in the glove compartment and go to sleep on these occasions was suddenly replaced by the cold professional who is in charge of things and knows what he's about.

'I don't know why you're feeling so pleased with yourself –
a five-year-old child would have . . . '

'Up yours, Frederick.'

I strode purposefully over to the garage workshop and asked them if they could lend me a thingummybob for removing hub-caps – it impresses them no end if you know the correct terminology.

'Course you can,' said the motor mechanic with a willingness that could have had him thrown out of the union, and within a couple of minutes I was back on my knees beside the car.

First I took the skin off my knuckles and then I forced the hub-cap off the wheel. It bounced twice and rolled under the car. I fished it out but there was no key taped to the inside.

Strange. I remembered tucking it into a little plastic packet to keep it dry and then strapping it in position with roughly three-quarters of a mile of adhesive tape. I'm very thorough.

'Must be the rear wheel,' I thought, although I could remember taping it to this very hub-cap as clear as day.

I was prizing away like mad when I heard the man say something. I didn't quite catch it the first time because the rear hub-cap was a much tougher proposition altogether and it was putting up a hell of a fight.

'What exactly do you think you're doing?'

I couldn't shift it – I had it almost bent in two by now but it was still far more attached to its moorings than it was to me.

I looked up and there above me stood a man and his wife and the petrol pump attendant.

'I've taped a spare key to the hub-cap,' I explained. 'I dropped the other one inside . . .'

And then I stopped, because in the car at the next pump I could see Aileen opening and shutting her mouth like a goldfish as she sang along happily with the radio. Light opera by the look of it – she was conducting an invisible orchestra and had her chin tucked well down on her chest.

'I'm sorry – I thought this was my car.'

The man and his wife and the petrol pump attendant took a long look at my car and then turned back to the one I was stripping.

My car is red – this one was green. My car is a neat little Lancia sports – this one was a Volvo estate that went on and on for ever.

My car had Aileen inside, she was building to a crescendo now and about to bring in the third violin who was waiting patiently by the clutch pedal. This car had two small children in the back, staring through the window wondering what the hell this man was doing pinching their daddy's hub-caps.

'I thought this was my car,' I repeated, rather lamely this time.

'They're a lot alike,' agreed the man, with just a touch of sarcasm I thought.

'I'll just get these back on for you.'

I slammed on the front hub-cap and then bent back the other as best I could before the wheel started spinning in front of me and the Volvo roared away from the pumps.

'It's been one of those days,' I told the attendant.

'I bet you have a lot of them,' he said.

I needed a rest and to see a friendly face before I started again and so, as Aileen was milking the applause and taking her third bow from an ecstatic audience, I slipped into the driving seat beside her.

'I've just taken the hub-cap off the Volvo – the one that was parked in front of us.'

'Did you find the key?'

'No of course I didn't – why would it be stuck to his hub-cap?'

'Why did you take it off then?'

I tried to explain, but there really is no explanation as to why I ravel life's simple tasks into such a Gordian knot. My mind and body seem to travel on different planes – rather like the Royal family.

As my body is passing by Peterborough on the A1,

my mind is already up on the M62 wondering why they always have the fast lane out of commission if it's the heavy lorries that cause all the damage.

Or why is it that at dusk the drivers of the black cars you can't see very well are always the last ones to switch their lights on?

You see, I'm doing it again.

My daughter Sally rang that night from Brighton – she's very pregnant and I worry about her a lot. It's too far for me to rush with lots of hot water.

'How's the book going, Dad?'

'I've just finished chapter three.'

'What's it about?'

'Well – Aileen and I go to Currys to buy a television.'

'What happens then?'

'We come back.'

'How do you write a whole chapter about that?'

'God only knows.'

CHAPTER FOUR

Thermal sat on the speaker and cocked an ear to the muffled tones of the man on Radio Leeds. Presenters are often accused of speaking through the back of their necks – this one had no idea he was speaking through a cat's bottom.

'. . . at EuroDisney. So now let's have a look at the original article over there in Florida.'

He paused, either for dramatic effect or to spit out the cat hairs, and I wondered what the local connection would be.

We had already been whisked off to the Algarve for a winter break and gone topless in St Tropez, but local radio must have its local link even on a holiday programme, and the hard money would be resting on Holmfirth and the *Last of the Summer Wine* country.

Thermal eased himself into mid-air as I opened the fridge door and the presenter took the opportunity to clear his throat. No milk bottles this morning, just a two-litre carton lying on its side, and Thermal sat down again with a sigh of disappointment.

Every morning we have a running battle to see who's going to get the top of the milk, and you know where it is with a bottle – you can see it, it's up at the top. But where is it when a two-litre carton of milk has been lying on its side overnight? I suppose it must be on the side that's uppermost, but when you stand the carton upright, how long does it take to float to the top?

Thermal and I are both busy men. I have the papers to read and he has the postman to savage and we can't be bothered with such things. I stood the carton on the chopping board and it told me to 'Open other side'.

It always does. I can't ever remember a time when I stood a carton upright and it said, 'Who's a clever boy then?'

Ever since these damn cartons invaded our supermarket shelves I have been turning them round and opening them from the other side – it must be about twenty-five years now. Twenty-five years of revolving a cardboard box every morning just because they are designed to come out of the fridge the wrong way round.

'Go on,' I thought, 'break the rules for once,' and I took hold of the carton by its ears.

'Don't . . .' warned the man on the radio, and I paused in mid-rip.

'. . . think you have to travel halfway across the world for the holiday of a lifetime.'

I relaxed once more and, taking a fresh grip on the carton, I joined in, in my best BBC voice.

'No – you don't even have to leave Yorkshire to savour the many delights of Holmfirth and the *Last of the Summer Wine* country.'

Thermal nodded. He also had his pocket-money on Compo and company.

'Bradford is the place to be,' declared the presenter. 'You don't even have to leave Yorkshire to savour the many delights of Bradford.'

Thermal and I stared at one another in disbelief.

'Bradford?'

'Yes, Bradford, surprisingly enough,' he went on. 'The town is fast gaining a reputation as one of Britain's premier tourist resorts.'

Who would have guessed it? Bradford – the land of a thousand take-aways. Never mind, better luck next time, and I turned my attention back to the carton. It was leaning up against the toaster, wearing its wax jacket with all the uppercrust smugness of a public schoolboy whose daddy owned the dairy.

'When I say other side – I mean, other side.'

'Stuff you,' I thought.

I pushed the two tabs back, stuck my fingernail down the top flap – and it opened just like that. I waited for a moment, to see if the milk would come boiling over the top just to teach me a lesson, but it didn't.

I tried pouring it into Thermal's saucer, half expecting it might pour at right angles or something just to show me you shouldn't go interfering with nature, but it didn't.

In twenty-five years I had never opened a carton with any real success until this morning.

I grinned at Thermal and he grinned at me, punching his paw in the air to celebrate my success.

'What would you say,' asked the man on Radio Leeds, 'is the reason for Bradford's 147 per cent increase in tourism?'

Well, Thermal didn't know and I didn't know, but the man from the Council was in no doubt.

'It's the workin' horses, in't it?'

'The working horses?'

'Oh aye.' His voice wore a brown gaberdine suit and the trousers were just an inch too short. 'They've been a great success, have the workin' horses.'

Thermal spluttered into his milk and I patted his back. The milk carton gaped vacantly at the kettle, shoulders drooping along with his ego – all this was way above his head. The man on Radio Leeds pulled himself together.

'And you think this increase is all due to the working horses?'

'Well – perhaps not all,' the brown suit conceded. 'We have renovated a couple of back-to-back houses as well.'

'Have you?'

'Oh aye – it's been quite a draw.'

Thermal and I went for a shower. I go in the cubicle, he waits outside and sits on the bath-mat to make sure it's still there when I come out.

Poor old Walt Disney must be turning in his grave. All that money spent in France when just a couple of working Mickey Mouses and the renovation of a back-to-back castle would have done the trick.

I reached for a towel and stepped out on to the warm patch Thermal had been cooking for me. He popped in for a paddle up at the shallow end.

What a nice day – and I had a feeling it was going to get even better.

And it did. I was ironing Aileen's silk camisole when the call came through from Brighton. It was my favourite camisole, the one which is a lot more see-through than she realizes – all of which must make *you* realize that female emancipation has taken immense strides in our house.

I took the call at my ironing board and answered in a brisk, business-like manner. With the portable phone parked on one end, the ironing board can be switched instantly from pressing camisoles to pressing business. Had there been enough space along its length I would have added my leather blotter and a photograph of the wife and kids.

'Hello – board room.'

'Hi, Dad.'

The sound of my daughter's voice immediately transformed this tough no-nonsense executive into the sort of father every girl should have – loving, caring, and a million miles away from the man who, seconds before, had steeled himself to deal with the outrageous demands of his wily publisher.

'Is everything all right?'

'Yes – fine. The contractions have started, so I'm just off to the hospital.'

I'm good at this sort of thing – at calming people down. The years of experience with her mother, in hospital after

45

hospital, have given me an inner peace which serves as a
gentle, soothing balm to those I massage with my rich
brown voice.

'Right! Now then – the thing is . . . Are you on your
own? It's the hospital, you see . . . Is Steve with you?
What about your waters – shouldn't they be breaking or
something? Ring for an ambulance right away. Do it now,
I'll hang on. No, you can't, can you – not while I'm on the
phone. I'll hang up. Better still – I'll ring the hospital.
What's the number? Give me the code for Brighton.'

I don't panic when it comes to dealing with a crisis and
it had the desired effect. Sally sounded almost serene as she
told me of the arrangements she had made, speaking to me
slowly as though to a small child. I suppose motherhood
must be seeping through her veins already.

'Don't worry, Dad. Steve's on his way and I'm all
packed. It'll be hours yet. Will you be driving down?'

'Yes. In the car. I shall be driving down in the car.
Let's see, three-hundred miles – I can do that in . . .'

'There's no rush. Just take your time.'

'I shall come down in the car.'

'It would be best – if you're driving.'

I told her how much I loved her and then went to
tell Aileen the good news. For her the baby had got its
timing all wrong, she and her camisole were off teaching
at a writer's school for the next three days and there was
no way she could be in Brighton at the same time.

'How is she?'

'Fine – I calmed her down.'

'Good. Tell her I'm thinking of her?'

'Of course I will.'

'And ring me as soon as you have any news.'

The traffic on the M1 was pretty light. The man who
drives the Citroën 2CV in the fast lane between Leeds
and Derby on even dates was up and about again. You
will be pleased to hear that he was looking extremely well,
his signalling has improved somewhat and he appears to
have had the car serviced – he got it up to around 25

mph at one point. I waved to him as I passed him on the inside – I think he's lonely.

Even though I had the motorway more or less to myself, and the few fellow travellers I did come across were all going in the same direction, it seemed to take me hours before I reached junction 29.

I should be doing something constructive, I thought, so I switched off the radio and got down to some serious thinking. I was getting behind with this book of mine. My year in Huddersfield had come to a full-stop in mid February.

I reached over to the passenger seat for a Dunhill International. I can't think without a cigarette, but it began to look as though I might have to learn very quickly as my seat-belt held me in a vice-like grip and kept me pinned to the back of the seat.

Junction 28 had come and gone by the time I worked myself loose, rocking and rolling, backwards and forwards, until the belt allowed itself to run free once more.

It was then that the flashback came to me. The day that seat-belts became compulsory, it must have been all of ten years ago now. This book was going to be one long flashback. What the hell – I had two hundred and fifty miles ahead of me. I deserved a flashback.

FEBRUARY (continued)

To be honest, I didn't realize I had any in my car. It took me ages to find them. Fancy sticking the seat-belts halfway up the door frame. It was the one place I would never have dreamed of looking, and when I did find them I thought – 'These are never long enough.'

There was just this little belt, about three inches long with a chrome buckle hanging on one end. There was no way it was going to fit me.

I looked them up in the handbook, which wasn't easy since most of it was in German, and eventually I discovered that what I had was a matching pair of inertia-reel seat-belts and they were supposed to be only three inches long – but they stretched.

Well, mine didn't at first. I yanked like mad but it wouldn't budge. Then it dawned on me that you had to coax them out gently, and an hour and a half later I found myself sitting in the driving seat, strapped in, with the buckle bit stuck in the thing that's welded to the floor. (I hope I'm not getting too technical for you.)

Apparently they were the latest thing, these inertia-reel seat-belts. They had been designed to ride with you so that you could lean forward to the dashboard and break a lump off your Yorkie Bar – or reach right over to the passenger-well to pick up your Yorkie Bar when you've gone round a corner and it's done a double somersault off the dashboard.

They are designed to work properly only when yanked – when you perform a proper emergency stop – so I thought I would give it a try.

I parked the car in the drive, sat behind the wheel, took a deep breath and slammed my whole body forward, as though I had crashed into something rather nasty.

It didn't quite work out the way I had expected. The seat-belt came with me and I smashed the bridge of my nose right against the top of the steering wheel, and it doesn't half hurt when you smash the bridge of your nose against the top of the steering wheel.

There was blood everywhere. All down the front of the cashmere sweater I was supposed to save only for best. And there's another snag with seat-belts.

You try getting your handkerchief out of your right-hand trouser pocket. You can't get in – you have to lean over sideways and balance on one cheek while you drip blood all over the passenger seat.

I thought, 'This seat-belt must be a bit too heavy on the inertia.' I decided to test it scientifically in an ongoing, on-the-road situation.

And so, with a lump of cotton-wool stuck up each nostril, I ventured out on to the highway, and after revving up to sixty miles an hour I took another deep breath and slammed on the brakes.

It worked beautifully. The wheels locked solid and the car slewed only slightly out of line before shuddering to a grinding halt within yards. The seat-belt gripped me in an iron clasp and my head hardly left the headrest.

The cotton-wool plug dropped out of my left nostril, but other than that there were hardly any ill effects whatsoever. My right nipple was ever so slightly bruised, but that's the price we test pilots have to pay.

The whole operation was perfectly executed. Perhaps the man driving the lorry a few yards behind me wouldn't have agreed – he must have had kittens.

I suppose I should have glanced in my rear-view mirror before slamming on the brakes – but then I wouldn't have been able to do that if it had been a real emergency such as a vole crossing the road, something that called for really desperate measures such as that.

I could hear his brakes squealing and smell his tyres burning as I tried to poke the cotton-wool plug out from under the handbrake. Through the rear-view mirror I could see his load swaying and his back end slewing round to have a word with his front end, but I had my eyes tightly shut as he finally wrestled the lorry to a halt, sideways, just inches from my back bumper.

I was about to get out of the car so that I could explain just why I had stopped so abruptly, but then I decided against it when I saw that both he and his mate had jumped down from the cab and were coming to have a word with me.

I drove off. It's not that I am a coward, you understand, it's just that I never know what to say on these occasions. Besides, I'd bled enough for one day.

The stroll down memory lane had helped the miles to roll away, and before I knew it the Blue Boar service station was only half a mile ahead.

The M1 has a strange effect on me. I ache for a service station and a cup of hot coffee and then, as the signs cut down the distance from a mile to half a mile, and then begin to count down from three dashes to one, I find myself ignoring the slip-road with a steely determination.

'I'll see if I can get another fifty miles under my belt.'

It doesn't happen on the A1. I could show you where the toilets are in every Little Chef between Middlesborough and London wearing a blindfold.

But on the M1 I feel I have an obligation to the authorities. They have paved three lanes of rural England in more or less a straight line, especially so that I can be in the capital in double quick time, and it doesn't seem fair to go mucking about.

It's as though I am wearing a hair shirt, and by the time I arrive in London I have a pious glow of self-righteousness about me that a Jehovah's Witness would kill for.

But not today. Today I wanted to phone the hospital in Brighton – I might be a grandfather by now and I needed to know.

Grandfathers do things differently. For a start, I would have to lower the driving seat in the car – when you are driving behind a grandfather you only ever see the top of his head – and I must buy some boiled sweets to carry loose in my pocket. I wondered if they sold picnic baskets here as well.

I would buy a bonnet for Aileen in Brighton and tell her to do a few buttons up – you can't go having a grandmother with cleavage. She would probably argue that she was a wicked step-grandmother and that it was expected of her, but at least she could start wearing a bra.

It seemed to take ages before the hospital answered the phone, and then I waited again to be transferred to the ward. A nurse listened patiently and then disappeared.

'I'll go and find out what's happening.'

What did she mean, go and find out? If my grandchild had been born already then the sound of church bells would be ringing throughout the length and breadth of

Brighton. And if not, a highly-trained squad of para-
medics would be camped by Sally's bedside with a ton
and a half of sophisticated equipment. What did she mean,
go and find out?

'Mr Longden?'

'Yes.'

'I have your son-in-law here.'

'Steve – what's happening, Steve?'

There was the sound of a phone being passed from one
to another, a slight pause for a deep breath and then the
voice of a man who was not from this planet.

'She's got fingernails and everything.'

'The baby? It's born?'

'. . . fingernails and everything.'

'Is she a girl?'

'She's beautiful.'

'And Sally?'

'She's had a bad time – but she's going to be all
right.'

'Thank God for that – I'll be with you soon.'

'I'll get back to Sally now.'

'You're sure they are both all right?'

'. . . fingernails and everything.'

The nurse took over.

'She's seven and a half pounds, Mr Longden, and they
are both going to be fine.'

I rang Aileen straight away but she was out – she must
be on her way to the university. I told the answering machine all about it, but it has no soul and I'd
give it a piece of my mind when I got back home. I
would have to wait until Brighton before I could tell
Aileen.

I filtered back in amongst the mass of bodies who
were playing slot machines, buying papers and eating
burgers. I felt so happy and relieved and I thought of
Steve and his fingernails and everything.

My son-in-law, the karate expert who was as hard as
nails and yet so loving and gentle with Sally. He'd make

a wonderful father – I wouldn't like to be one of the young men who came chasing after my granddaughter.

I hoped Sally was all right. I didn't like to think of her in pain – and then I began to cry with the relief of it all.

Men are allowed to cry on occasions such as this, but it doesn't help matters if you are in the middle of a service area on the M1. The tears ran silently down my cheeks as I stalked through the crowd towards the car park, although I could swear I heard them splashing as they hit the concrete.

I wanted to tell somebody, but it had to be somebody who cared and they were in short supply around here – and then I found a man who did.

'Have you ever thought of joining the AA, sir?'

'I'm a member already.'

'I thought you looked the sensible sort the moment I saw you.'

I smiled and carried on – and then on impulse I turned back.

'I've just become a grandfather.'

'Oh that's wonderful, sir – just?'

'I rang up from in there.'

'I see – and is it a boy or a girl, sir?'

'It's a girl – seven and a half pounds, she's got finger-nails and everything.'

'And the mother – is she all right?'

'She's fine.'

He dipped into his coat pocket and produced a wallet.

'Oh that's good. There's something magical about a baby girl – I remember I had a good cry as well. Would you care to have a look at a photograph of my granddaughter, sir? She's nearly three months now, her name is . . .'

The AA can relax as far as I am concerned. They don't have to include me in any more of their £100,000 draws and I wouldn't dream of accepting a free gift from such close friends. They've got me hooked – I'm theirs for life.

*   *   *

52

In Brighton I found the hospital. It was in bits and pieces all over the place, but they had the maternity unit hidden in another bit altogether and it took some tracking down.

Parking the car was impossible. I thought of selling it, but eventually I found a space just outside Eastbourne and set out on the long walk back for a spot of grandfather bonding.

This was very important, and I started with a distinct handicap. Grandfather and grandmother French had the home advantage, they lived here, and I could be playing away for the rest of my life.

Graham had already brought Steve's old bucket and spade down from out of the attic with the intention of taking my granddaughter to the beach this very summer. I couldn't compete with that, and Pam had been wonderful with Sally throughout what had been a very difficult pregnancy.

They would be on hand, day after day, and I would just be that old man up north – you know, the one with the grey beard who you go up and see once a year. Of course you remember him.

It was a good job I had a soft spot for them – I could have been very jealous. They would be able to see her regularly, be available for babysitting at short notice, and if Sally went back to work she could always leave the baby with the Frenchs . . . Oh I don't know – maybe living up in Yorkshire wasn't such a bad idea after all.

I could be the alternative grandfather, the one she would always want to come and stay with, as she matured into a ravishing young woman.

'Of course you can sleep with your boyfriend – just don't tell your mother.'

The thought gave me a spring in my step and I fairly bounced into the hospital.

There were curtains around the bed and you can't knock on curtains. I pulled them apart an inch or so but the bed was empty. Perhaps they had been taken off for more tests or something.

I sat on the edge of the bed and waited. There was an empty cot on the other side, a rather clinical cot, functional – not a bit like the one with the drapes that Sally had.

I went over to examine it more closely. There was a baby in this empty cot, all tucked up and fast asleep. It was the most beautiful baby and I wanted to pick her up, but I daren't – she might break.

'We're calling her Katie.'

Sally stood behind me, a towel over her shoulder and a toilet bag in her hand. Her eyes sparkled but the rest of her was absolutely shattered.

'Steve's having the next one.'

I gave her a very careful hug and then helped her pull the curtains back to reveal a dozen other beds, all with the same antiseptic cot pulled up by the side.

As she climbed painfully back between the sheets I cast an eye over the other occupants of the ward. I would have thought they would have been terribly jealous of how pretty Katie was, but surprisingly they all seemed quite happy with their own babies. It's a funny world.

As Sally told me of the last few hours, I curled my finger in Katie's palm and stroked the back of her tiny hand gently with my thumb. She was absolutely beautiful – she had fingernails and everything.

CHAPTER FIVE

March came in like the cowardly lion. It flew into a tantrum every now and then and threw in the odd hailstone for good measure, but on the whole it just huffed and puffed for a while and then sat on its backside and waited for April to take over.

Aileen came out of her self-imposed exile with yet another book to her credit, a thriller this time, and as soon as she had become accustomed to the light she set off on the Luncheon Club circuit.

The Ladies Luncheon Clubs are very well organized and provide a good meal, a large appreciative audience and some pleasant company on the top table. They also pay their speakers on the nail, which is very much appreciated.

There are the exceptions, of course, and we found one of them just south of Birmingham. Madam Chairman introduced Aileen in a soft Scottish brogue that owed more to Edinburgh than it did to the Black Country.

'I would like you to meet Miss Aileen Armitage. She's written twenty-nine novels – she's awfully promiscuous.'

Aileen leaned over to me and whispered behind her hand.

'How did she know that?'

I was still suffering from a surfeit of hats down in the West Country the week before. It is only to be expected that one or two of the older ladies in the audience will be wearing hats, but when it looks more like Ascot Week out there, then it's time to head for the hills.

'Ladies, if you would please turn your chairs round to face our speaker,' the President had asked them, but they wouldn't dream of doing anything so vulgar.

I was twenty minutes into my allotted hour before I achieved my first laugh and by that time I was seriously considering disembowelling myself with the butter knife.

From that moment on things improved considerably, and there were feathers and veils shaking all over the place by the time I had finished. The President apologized to me.

'Don't mind them laughing at you – I'm sure they enjoyed it.'

I was sitting on a low wall in the car park afterwards, smoking a cigarette and wondering why I hadn't noticed the time-warp on the way down, when one of the ladies strolled over to have a word with me.

'They tell me you get paid for doing this?'

'Yes, that's right.'

'Well I never.'

And with that she turned on her heels and marched off towards her chauffeur and a large Bentley. I stubbed out my cigarette and kicked myself for having left the butter knife on the table.

Aileen was having no trouble with her audience, she had them in the palm of her hand, so I was able to relax and study Madam Chairman at close quarters.

I was sure I had seen her before, that face – the way it moved as though every muscle had to think hard about what it was supposed to do next before it did it.

Just as Aileen was winding up I got it. Maggie Smith

as Jean Brodie – she was the spitting image, even down to the accent. She rose to introduce the vote of thanks.

'Miss Armitage, that was wonderful. Tell me something – you had a very unhappy first marriage and four children, then you lost your sight and started writing. You went out into the world on your own, wrote twenty-nine novels, won the Woman of the Year Award and now you are happily married to Deric. Have you ever thought of writing your autobiography?'

Aileen rose to her feet.

'Well, I have thought about it,' she said, 'but a lot of people might get hurt – perhaps it would be best if it were published posthumously.'

Miss Brodie smiled encouragingly.

'Well, make it soon, Miss Armitage – make it soon.'

We drove home the pretty way. I wanted to show Aileen Chatsworth Park, and so we side-stepped Derby, cut off through Kedleston and headed towards Matlock, my old home town.

'That's the entrance to Kedleston Hall,' I pointed out as we passed by.

She stared out of the window, not seeing a thing.

'Oh – very nice.'

Our friends ask us why we rarely travel abroad – you would enjoy it, they say, but I just imagine the two of us looking down on one of the modern wonders of the world.

'*There you are, Aileen, that's the Grand Canyon.*'

'*Oh – very nice.*'

It wouldn't be worth it. When we visit those old satanic mills that are dotted all over West Yorkshire, even though these days they are mostly locked and barred and only shadows of their former selves, Aileen can almost taste the atmosphere, almost touch the past that is hidden deep in those damp walls.

If you close your eyes tight you can see the ragged children labouring at their looms, hear the hooter sounding at the end of a long shift and watch them set out, exhausted, on the journey home.

But scenery is a different matter. Scenery can be very boring without the pictures.

Matlock Bath seemed surprised to see us. It hadn't expected visitors this early in the year and it was at a loss as to what to do with us. Shop doors creaked from a winter's warping and the shop windows still had a dull, half-baked look about them as they tried to pull themselves together and show some interest.

There was a time when Matlock was famous as a spa town, and in those days elegant ladies in their ball-gowns and their menfolk in formal evening dress would parade through the streets, taking the air before dinner as the natives perched on the low stone walls and gawped at them.

These days Matlock Bath is all black leather and Kawasaki motor bikes. Blue jeans and brightly coloured T-shirts blossom briefly in the summertime, but anoraks and thick sweaters are the hardy annuals. Formal is if your jeans have button flies and casual is so relaxed that it's a wonder it doesn't keep falling over.

I have seen the Parade so jam-packed with brightly coloured anoraks that, from high in the surrounding hills, it looked as though a giant tube of Smarties had been spilled over the town.

But today just a few bikers strutted their stuff, like an advance guard from another planet in their leather suits and smoked visors, and a putty-coloured anorak walked a putty-coloured dog slowly past a Gents' toilet that should have been condemned way back in Roman times.

I wanted to show Aileen the shop I owned some years ago. It was down at the end of a pretty alleyway. There had been other pretty shops and an Italian restaurant run by George and Cynthia who had turned spaghetti bolognese into an Anglo-Saxon art form.

But things had changed and my old shop had now been carved up into smaller units. I tried to explain just how it had been in the old days, and Aileen listened and nodded intelligently every now and then, but it wasn't working, and so we strolled down the street for a while until we came across a shy little café, hidden away behind a pair of grey net curtains.

A bunch of bikers sat at one table, with their helmets dumped upside down on the floor beside them begging for scraps. They talked quietly and knowledgeably of BSAs and Harley Davidsons while their leather suits conducted a running argument with the upholstery on the plastic benches. They seemed very pleasant and they smiled at us as we walked in.

A family of three sat at another table, their heads bowed over knickerbocker glories, three long spoons scooping up the multi-coloured ice-cream with a synchronized precision that made it seem like a team event. I ordered two coffees and then took another look at them.

There was no doubt about it, she was a great one for knitting, was the mother. All three of them wore identical cardigans, double-breasted, with rebellious roll-neck collars, and finished off with those old-fashioned leather buttons, each one about the size of a small walnut.

She must have bought the wool in a job-lot and it was the sort of green that you might find growing on a gravestone in a very wet cemetery.

The little boy would be about seven years old and his cardigan seemed to have a life of its own. No doubt he would grow into it by the time he was forty-three, but for the moment it looked as though it had swallowed him whole.

The mother seemed to be obsessed with cuffing him about the side of the head and I couldn't understand why. He was sitting as quiet as a mouse and behaving himself impeccably – it was his cardigan that wouldn't sit still.

He only had to cough and it would leap into action, running wildly up and down his arms and then screwing itself up round his neck until his little head disappeared completely. Then his mother would yank it out with her bare hands and cuff it once more.

It upset me. I don't like to see kids being ill-treated, but there's little you can do in such a situation. Interfere and he might get a double dose once they were outside. I just had to hope that one day his cardigan would revert to the wild and go straight for her throat.

'Kill,' I muttered under my breath.

'Pardon?'

'Nothing. I was just talking to that little boy's cardigan over there.'

Aileen took a deep breath and shook her head sadly. I don't suppose I'm the only man whose wife doesn't understand him.

The coffee was far better than we had any right to expect it to be and we were halfway through the second pot when the bikers got to their feet and began to leave.

The Queen's Own Emerald Cardigans had been watching their every move, and after the last bit of leather had squeezed itself out on to the pavement the father snorted and muttered to himself.

'Yobbos.'

The mother agreed.

'What do they think they look like?'

She gave her offspring a final cuff around the earhole and then the three of them lined up in single file and made for the door.

As they passed by our table I caught a glimpse of their backs for the first time and saw the large letters that this arbiter of good taste had embroidered on their cardigans in bright yellow silks.

First DADDY BEAR squeezed his way through the narrow aisle with MUMMY BEAR following on close behind, her ample hips shoving our sugar bowl halfway across the table.

BABY BEAR was the last in line, ruefully rubbing his earhole as his little legs tried desperately to match his cardigan stride for stride.

As they reached the doorway the cardigan stood back and let him go through first. I thought that was rather a nice touch. At least he had one friend who might help him on his journey through this cruel world.

As we drove on through Matlock itself, over the bridge and into Crown Square, I pointed out the places that I knew would interest Aileen.

'That's where I used to do my banking.'

'That's where I got my papers from.'

'That's where I got knocked down by a truck.'

I thought that at least this last item might spark off a little reaction, but when I glanced across I saw that she had reclined her seat until it was horizontal and closed her eyes for a nap.

I turned the car left on to the Bakewell road and headed for Chatsworth Park, and very soon the Whitworth Cottage Hospital came up on my right.

'That's where I had my knee stitched.'

This riveting slice from my former life rated nothing more than a sleepy grunt from my travelling companion, but it didn't really matter – I thought it was fascinating stuff.

I love Chatsworth Park. As the car drilled over the first cattle grid I felt the peace of the place descend upon me once more.

I used to bring my problems here when it all became too much for me. I would sit very still, watching the sheep going about their business and the deer grazing on the far hills. The problems would still be waiting for me when I returned home, but I would be stronger somehow after soaking in this gentleness for an hour or so.

I swung the car off the road and came to a halt at the top of a grassy slope. The park lay spread out beneath me, dotted all over with more sheep than I had ever seen here before. It must be their annual general meeting.

They all seemed to have a couple of lambs apiece and I love lambs, I think they are the most charming of animals. There were white ones and black ones – all of them jumping up and down and barking or braying or whatever it is that little lambs do. The entire park looked as though it had been sprayed with tiny pullovers.

Aileen must see this. Even if scenery was a blank wall to her eyes, when it teemed with life like this I could paint it for her in vivid colours.

She was lying in state, her hands folded across her chest. I tapped her on the shoulder.

'Aileen, wake up – we're here, in Chatsworth Park.'

Her voice came up from the dead, thick with sleep, and her eyelids fluttered briefly as she considered the invitation.

'Oh – very nice.'

She mustn't miss this, it was wonderful. Perhaps we could have a walk and pat a few lambs, they looked tame enough. I had a cauliflower and some carrots in the boot – do lambs eat carrots?

'Aileen, come on – you'll love this, all these sheep and their lambs – I think it's a parent-teachers' evening.'

She stirred slightly and lifted herself up on to her elbows.

'I was a school governor in Walsall.'

'Yes I know you were – but that's not what I'm talking about.'

She slid back down again, yawning as she went, and then turned over on her side.

'You have a word with them – ask them what they want.'

I sat quietly on the grass, my back up against the car door, and one by one all the lambs in the vicinity came over to have a look at me. They had been warned by their mothers not to take carrots from strange men, so I ate one myself and put the others back in the boot.

This morning we had set out early over the scrubby moors surrounding Huddersfield and there, pulling at the wiry grass, the sheep were still childless. It would be late April before they had any lambs and I thought how wonderful mother nature is.

She knows only too well that up there on the windswept hills the weather could be cruelly unpredictable for some time yet, whereas down here in Chatsworth Park it was mild and sunny, an overcoat warmer. And so she simply arranges things accordingly. Isn't that amazing?

I heard Aileen's limbs creak as she stretched herself and then her head appeared at the window.

'I could murder a cup of tea.'

As we headed home along Matlock Moor I turned the car into Brickyard Farm and headed towards a free cup of tea and maybe a sandwich or two.

George Statham's car was resting up outside his farmhouse and I didn't want to wake it. George is a dead ringer for Pavarotti, beard and all. He's approaching twenty stone from the wrong direction and not getting all that close. His car has all the cares of the world upon its axles and my heart went out to it as it leaned up against a wall and snoozed in the pale evening light.

I parked up close so that, when it came to, it could have a heart to heart with my Lancia. It's a good listener even if it is an Italian.

George gave me a bear hug and I consoled myself with the thought that my shoulder might go back in on its own if I stuck to light duties and rested up for a fortnight or so.

He once fought Brian London in the boxing ring and I think Brian London was very brave.

Beryl asked us if we would like a cup of tea.

'Well, only if you are making . . .'

'Yes please,' said Aileen.

She gave George a big kiss for all his help with a book she had been working on. He had been her official advisor on farming in general and pigs in particular and now she wanted to know all about tractors around the time of the First World War. She gets very good value for one of her kisses.

I waited until they each took a breath at the same time and then leapt in with my philosophical thought for the day.

'Isn't nature wonderful?'

'How do you mean?'

I told him about the sheep in Chatsworth Park and then about the sheep on the moors up in Yorkshire.

'Don't be so daft – it's nothing to do with nature.'

And then he told me the whole story and believe me it's absolutely disgusting.

I couldn't wait to get home and later that night I sat at my trusty Amstrad and began to write it down. Or rather write it up I suppose, since the words clung vertically to the screen in front of me.

MARCH

The whole damn business is engineered by the farmers and what they do is this. They get hold of a young innocent ram and tell him all about the facts of life – probably show him a magazine or two where sexy pouting ewes in living colour have been sheared in provocative places – and then they set him loose in Chatsworth Park.

Can you imagine it? There are four thousand ewes scattered all over the place, idly nibbling the grass and wondering whether or not to stay in that night and wash their hair, when all of a sudden a Land Rover pulls up and two big burly shepherds toss poor little Walter right in the middle of them.

No introductions – nothing. Off goes young Walter, chasing over hundreds of acres with the sole intention of making mad passionate love to each and every ewe in sight whether he fancies them or not. I find it very hard to believe that the Duchess of Devonshire knows anything about this – she'd put her foot down, I'm sure she would.

He doesn't get commission and he's not on time and a half or anything like that, and after a day and a night

64

of ewe after ewe telling him that she's got one of her headaches coming on, it suddenly dawns on him that he still has three and a half thousand to go.

At this point they send out the Land Rover to pick him up – he doesn't take much catching, he's just standing there cross-eyed and groggy – and then they take him back to the farmhouse where they give him a mug of hot cocoa and a digestive biscuit and a couple of days later he's back on nights again.

Now something was puzzling me and I put the question to George . . .

'How do they know which of the ewes have been caught and which have been too fast on their feet for him?'

It seemed a reasonable question to me. I mean they can't spend days scouring Chatsworth Park to see which of the ewes have a silly grin on their faces and which ones haven't, can they?

George gave me one of those looks that farmers reserve for the likes of me and said,

'Raddle bags.'

'I beg your pardon?'

'You heard.'

It seems that what they do is this. They fit a harness to the ram's chest with a little bag attached. It's called a raddle bag. They strap it on tight and fill it full of red paint so that when the ram's chest comes in contact with the ewe's back it leaves a big red blob.

Then, after he's had his rest and his mug of cocoa and his digestive biscuit, the next time they send him out they fill the bag with blue paint and that way they can tell when the lambs are due to be born.

And to think I thought it was all due to mother nature being so wonderful, when in fact there's this ram running all over Chatsworth Park with three and a half pints of emulsion paint strapped to his chest.

They call it tupping and it's so sordid. I always assumed that the red blobs meant that those sheep belonged to Farmer Smith and those with blue blobs to Farmer Jones.

It's the lambs I feel sorry for. Pity the poor soul who gets sniggered at by all the other little lambs because his mother is covered in red, blue, green and yellow blobs and everyone in the flock knows that she's no better than she ought to be.

I asked George what happened to the ewes who never got caught and he said that that was where your virgin wool came from.

I think he was joking.

CHAPTER SIX

The courtyard was beginning to look as though it belonged. Its predecessor had done a fine job for nigh on a hundred years but it had begun to show its age, and so last summer we had decided upon a fresh start.

'Raised beds, that's what you want,' the man from the landscape garden centre had said. 'Save you both a lot of trouble, not having to bend down at . . .'

He hesitated as he saw Aileen's fingers tighten around the handle of the dibber and watched as she measured the distance from the dibber to his throat, just waiting for him to say, 'at your age'.

'. . . at all,' he said.

A fortnight later he and his lad had delivered sixty wooden railway sleepers and stacked them by the back gate. They were each eight feet long, ten inches wide and five inches thick. The lad did most of the humping, presumably to eke out his war pension.

They were well-seasoned sleepers, obviously used to the rigours of an outdoor life and not frightened of hard work. They deserved a bit of peace in their retirement and we willingly paid for them in cash.

That night, on *Look North*, Harry Gration told us about the train crash just outside Halifax and I was on the phone to the garden centre before you could say the train now standing.

'It's nothing to do with your sleepers,' he told me.

'Are you sure?'

'I'm positive.'

I breathed a sigh of relief and apologized for even having thought of such an idea.

'They didn't say anything about one just outside Pontefract, did they?'

'No.'

'Well, that's all right then.'

I think it's best to deal with reputable traders – you can sleep at nights then.

Now, a year later, the sleepers had only to stand guard over a budding shrubbery and make sure the earth didn't move for anyone.

The cats believed that a giant scratching post had been lowered down from heaven, but the sleepers took it in their stride. I suppose once you've had the Yorkshire Pullman rattling across the back of your neck you tend to take *most* things in your stride.

Thermal had his claws stuck deep in the timber and his bum hoisted high in the April air, when my neighbour's voice rang out over the hedge.

Patrick had been born here in Huddersfield, but his accent had been flown over specially from County Cork just in time for his first birthday.

'You've made a fine cat out of him,' he said, 'I'll say that for you.'

Thermal had once belonged to Patrick – I had stolen him when he was only a kitten. I had been forgiven, but the guilt still surfaced now and then.

'They tell me,' he said, 'that you've written a book about him.'

'That's right – it's selling very well.'

He considered this for a moment or so.

'Aren't you worried people might think you're a bit of a wimp – writing a book about a cat?'

I considered that for a moment or so.

'No, I don't think so. You've known me for some time, Patrick – do you think I'm a wimp?'

He considered first the cat and then a large lump of rebellious privet. Finally he considered me and a large smile spread right across his face.

'To be honest – yes.'

I got my own back on those few weeds who had enough muscle to fight their way through the thick layer of forest bark. The landscaper had lagged the entire garden with a deep carpet of the stuff, and by the time the weeds struck sunlight they were absolutely knackered. I dug in deep with my trowel – wimp indeed. Thermal sat grinning at me from the back step.

'And you can stop that.'

'*What?*'

'You know very well.'

I plunged the trowel in once more and cut an intruder off at the ankles. Hang on a minute – this was a thistle. I'd better go and get my gardening gloves before I handled this one. Then I'd show him who was a wimp.

Aileen was out combing the darker recesses of Mrs Singh's second-hand furniture emporium, looking for a small corner table. I was to pick her up when the phone rang three times and until then I busied myself tidying up the kitchen.

The cats came in to help me, which was very nice of them. Thermal sat by the fridge door to make sure nothing escaped and Tigger sat by Thermal, ready to take over should an emergency arise. Arthur sat on Frink to keep her quiet. The silence was unnerving.

'You're not having anything.'

Tigger stared at Thermal and Thermal stared at Tigger. Arthur stared at me in amazement and Frink practised breathing in short bursts.

69

'It's not time for hours yet, so it's no good trying it on.'

The silence became even louder and the stillness almost crackled with a violent lack of activity.

I took the plates from the sink and laid them out to dry separately on the draining board so that the clash of china upon china wouldn't raise any false hopes.

'Five o'clock – then you can have something.'

Three pairs of eyes trained themselves on the back of my neck and a single, less experienced eye homed in from under Arthur's tail. Seven volts of neat willpower drilling through the air and boring little holes in my skull.

'All right then, just a snack – to keep you going.'

I heaved open the fridge door and as the light came on the tension in the kitchen went all slack at the edges and was replaced by a murmur of approval.

What a nice man.

Absolutely charming.

I've always said so.

As they chewed away together, all four jaws moving in close harmony, I packed the joint back in the fridge and took another look at Colin, our tame roll of Clingfilm.

He had sounded a bit wheezy as I tore off that last sheet and that wasn't a bit like Colin. He had the constitution of an ox and he usually pulled as hard at his end as I did at mine.

His tongue wasn't hanging out. He sat there on the worktop, as fat and friendly as always, but there was nothing sticking out between the two rows of jagged teeth.

I picked him up and he seemed strangely light. I shook him gently and he rattled. He couldn't have, could he? Not Colin?

With a knife I prised open the box out of which he had peered at us through his slit for more years than I care to remember. He'd seen it all, had Colin, and now there was nothing – just a cardboard tube rolling about aimlessly inside a big blue box.

I couldn't believe it. I carried him up to the office and sat him on my desk. That's where I'd found him ten years ago and now he had come full circle.

APRIL

The first time I laid eyes upon him he was sitting on a desk in a bankrupt clothing factory in Nottingham. They were selling off the effects and after years of writing on an ironing board in the bathroom I wanted something special for my new office.

There were several desks on offer. I would have loved the roll-top that Dickens might have tucked his knees underneath but they wanted far too much for that one.

I ignored the harsh steel tables. I couldn't afford to be too choosy but I had set my heart on one in warmest wood, with two or three small drawers on one side and a deep drawer on the other. It had appeared in my dreams time and time again as I put the final touches to the book I would probably never write.

And then I saw it, covered in dust in a far corner, and it was upon this desk that Colin perched.

At that time I didn't even know his name *was* Colin – I didn't even know it was a roll of Clingfilm. He was sealed in a large blue box that hung heavy with dust and cobwebs and I only had eyes for the desk.

'Tell you what,' said the man, 'I'll chuck this in as well,' and he popped Colin in the deepest drawer.

At home I took him out and cleaned him up. He was in a box about the size of a breadbin with a double row of neat teeth along one edge. He was enormous, he had been specially bred for the catering trade and he took us in his stride.

We had used him without thinking for about a year or so before we began to realize how remarkable he was, and then a little affection crept into our dealings with him.

We would say, 'Sorry, Colin,' as we forced the film

71

down gently on his lower jaw and then, 'Thank you, Colin,' as we tore off another sheet.

He was wound around huge turkeys and small chops. He withstood the intense heat of the microwave and the bitter cold of the freezer.

He could turn his hand to anything. When Sally almost chopped her finger off with the bread knife, Colin came up trumps as a bandage and he stopped the air getting at the burn when Nick leaned dreamily on the hot-plate.

He made sure that Bert the goldfish enjoyed a dignified funeral. Before Bert was lowered into the cold earth he was entombed in Clingfilm and very pretty he looked too – he hadn't looked anywhere near as good when he was swimming round and round in his bowl.

Colin saw great changes in our life. Wedding anniversaries, the children leaving home, my mother's seventy-fifth birthday party.

He caused one or two problems for my mother. She didn't see too well and she had never seen Clingfilm before in her life, and so perhaps we shouldn't have wrapped the individual pork pies separately.

She must have chewed away for at least five minutes before she gave up. Every time she took a bite – it bounced back.

'Funny crust that,' she said as she dropped it down on her plate and took out her revenge on a sausage roll.

Once the principle had been explained to her she went into Clingfilm in a big way and bought herself a mini-roll.

Her cat's life became a misery – nobody had ever taken the trouble to explain the principle to the cat, and he became a gibbering wreck every time he approached his saucer in the kitchen, wondering whether or not he would be able to get at it this time.

She once got her own back on my crabby Aunt Jessie by wrapping the soap in three layers of Clingfilm, and then sitting on the edge of the bath as the poor woman sat up to her chin in hot water and wondered why she couldn't get a lather out of her favourite bar of Lifebuoy.

When I moved to Huddersfield Colin came with me and it was a great comfort to know that he had been happy here. And now he was finished – a spent force.

I suppose he had a good innings. The average roll of Clingfilm can expect to last, at the very most, a few short months – and then only if he is in peak condition, gets to bed early at night and doesn't smoke.

But Colin had been with us, man and boy, for what seemed like forever and I couldn't bring myself to toss him casually in the dustbin. I didn't want him to end his days messy with wet teabags and custard, and so I took him out in the courtyard and laid him gently in the incinerator – a sort of funeral pyre.

Perhaps I should have waited until all the family could be here, but I didn't. I touched a match to him and waited by his side until all that remained of his very existence was a double row of metal teeth. We shall remember him – we shall never see his like again.

It's always the same, isn't it? As soon as you get to love them, they get run over by a bus.

The phone rang three times and I picked up my car keys – it rang a fourth time and I put them down and picked up the phone. It was Sally, and a baby bawled its lungs out in the background.

'Can you hang on a minute, Dad?'

I hung on for several minutes, wondering why she had rung me to tell me to hang on.

'Are you still there?'

'Yes, I'm still here.'

'Hang on a minute then.'

I hung on for a few minutes more – I was getting the hang of it by now.

'Dad?'

'Yes.'

'Oh good, you're still there.'

73

Katie bawled in the background once more – *she* was getting the hang of it as well.

'Hang on – I'm just going to shut the baby in a drawer.'

I always knew she would make a good mother. I waited and before I knew it she was back within the hour.

'Look, Dad, it's not really convenient at the moment. Can you ring me back tonight?'

'Yes of course I can.'

I apologized for troubling her and she said not to worry about it.

'Bye then.'

'Bye.'

I smiled to myself and wondered if my mother's spirit had been reborn in my daughter. God – what an awful thought.

The phone rang again a few seconds later – three times this time – and off I went to collect Aileen.

She had found herself a table, tucked away behind a burial mound of uncut moquette settees. How she finds anything I'll never know, she just has a nose for a bargain and she's never afraid to ask questions.

'Is this candlestick brass?'

'No – and it's a bayonet.'

She never minds how many times she gets it wrong. Anything smaller than a three-piece suite has to be fondled before she can recognize it. But she persists – it's the secret of her success and she's fantastic at it. I suppose I'm biased, but then everybody thinks she's fantastic and *they're* not. She could list for you right now every piece of stock in Mrs Singh's shop and take you straight to it.

She was very proud of her small corner table. It was sort of corner shaped and I thought she had found the perfect spot for it – in the corner. It could have been made for it, but she wasn't quite so sure.

'It's overshadowed by the sideboard, let's try the sideboard over there.'

I had to empty it before I could move it, but eventually I had it over there on the long wall, by the china cabinet. She shook her head.

'No – you can't see it there for the settee.'

Frink scooted past me bowling a napkin ring, so I tripped her up and took it off her.

'I've never been very keen on it – does it matter all that much if we can't see it?'

She gave me one of those looks that tells me to keep out of this because I don't know what I'm talking about, which I must admit is true most of the time.

I went and made us both a cup of tea and when I came back she had the settee jammed in the doorway.

'It's got to go, it's no good. Let's try the chesterfield from out of your office.'

Now I love having the chesterfield in my office. I can shut the door and have a long lie down if I want to and everybody thinks I'm working as long as I don't snore too loudly. There are times when I put my foot down and this was one of them.

It must have taken me ten minutes to wiggle it out of the office and into the hall. Aileen had convinced me that the settee was much the more comfortable of the two and after a trial snooze on both I was inclined to agree with her.

The only trouble was, having wiggled the chesterfield out, I couldn't wiggle the settee in, the doorway was too narrow, and I was about to burst into tears when she had an idea.

'We could take this one downstairs and bring the one from downstairs up here for your office – it is that bit smaller.'

The first rule of the removal business is that it can't be done by a committee. Somebody has to be in charge and I think the settee must have been downstairs before – it seemed to know what it was doing, anyway. It took the first bend like a veteran and then slowed slightly so I could catch up with it.

I jumped on board and we took the second bend together, with me leaning over like they do in sidecar racing. I think the settee appreciated having a professional as a partner and I certainly clipped several seconds off my personal best. Aileen was amazed.

'Did you carry it down all on your own?'

I tried not to catch the settee's eye as I shunted it into the lounge.

'Yes.'

I could swear I heard it snort, but settees aren't anywhere near as nippy on the flat as they are going downstairs and I was grunting so much by now that Aileen wouldn't have heard a thing.

'Patrick thinks I'm a wimp.'

I definitely heard Aileen snort as I told her about the cat book and she immediately leapt to my defence.

'I'd like to see Patrick carry a settee upstairs.'

Me too, I thought as I trundled number two out into the hall – preferably this one.

'At least it's much smaller than the other,' Aileen comforted me as she picked off the cushions one by one. 'It's good to get the worst over first, isn't it?'

Double mattresses go all silly when you try to pick them up. They are boneless articles and I can't be doing with them. Rolled up carpets pretend to be dead and don't help you one little bit. But settees, unless they are enjoying themselves tobogganing down a flight of stairs, are the most contrary of the lot.

They have no idea what they are supposed to do. They stick their elbows out as you try to work them round corners and the castors sprout high heels. This one was as thick as a bucket and it finished upside down with me underneath.

If it hadn't I might never have got it upstairs. I began to crawl upwards, like an upholstered turtle, one stair at a time, and to be quite honest I have never been so proud of myself in a long time.

It must have been an hour later before I had it tucked up in my office and I was having a practice lie down when Aileen said, 'That filing cabinet will have to go on the other wall and you can't have your desk under the window.'

She was right. I should have had to move the settee every time I wanted to open a drawer. So we shuffled the stuff around until we got it right.

I found my old typewriter in that sort of no man's land you create in a corner where two bookcases meet and you don't want to slot one behind the other. I hadn't seen it for years.

The very first story I wrote on this typewriter was the story about buying the typewriter itself – I waste very little – and if I remember rightly I sold it to the BBC.

I found it the same week I unearthed Colin and the desk, in a junk shop in Sheffield this time. The man's name was Reuben, I remember that, and he didn't like selling things.

I switched on the word processor, but it wasn't in the mood. Since I moved the desk the lead was now a yard and a half too short to reach the socket – I must do something about that.

The old typewriter gave a polite cough and for old time's sake I slipped off its jacket, rolled in a sheet of paper and began to pound the keys.

APRIL (continued)

It was tucked away to one side of the flyblown shop window and there was an upturned bluebottle out cold on the space bar – he must have done most of the blowing. The old man seemed rather reluctant to let me have a closer look at it.

'There's no ribbon in it.'

'I could buy a ribbon.'

'They're very special ribbons – half black, half red.'

'I've seen them – I can get those.'

A woman's voice from the back of the shop cut through the cobwebs.

'Reuben – show him the typewriter.'

Reuben sighed and pulled it from the window. The bluebottle fell off the space bar and dropped inside the works.

'It belonged to an army officer.' He shook his handkerchief at the typewriter, but the dust wasn't having any.

'How much do you want for it?'

He laid it down gently on a low blanket-box and stood back to admire it.

'He was savaged by his own Alsatian.'

There was a dent in one corner. The army officer must have dropped it as he was being savaged.

'How much do you want for it?'

'Ripped his throat out, it did.'

'Reuben!' The voice went up a notch this time and it wasn't taking any prisoners. 'Tell him how much.'

He shrugged and had another go with his handkerchief.

'Twenty pounds.'

'I'll give you fifteen.'

'He'll take it,' shouted the voice as it manifested itself through a bead curtain.

'He hates selling things.' She shook her head and held out her hand for the money. 'Can you imagine that? A shopkeeper who hates selling things?'

He winced as I made to pick it up and turned his back so that he wouldn't have to see it leave the shop.

'You got to have stock,' he said over his shoulder. 'An empty shop is bad for business.'

The woman shrugged as she held open the door for me and, so as not to cause him any more pain, I slipped away quietly – hugging to my bosom my brand-new second-hand typewriter and a free bluebottle.

That was nice, using the old typewriter again. It still had a touch of arthritis about it and its spelling hadn't improved any, but it had done me proud in the old days and I would leave it out on the long table so that it could feel a part of things.

Meanwhile I still had all the leads to my computer, printer, photo-copier and desk lamp to lengthen by roughly four and a half feet, and then there was that mountain of stuff from the sideboard waiting to be repatriated.

Aileen had been busy while I juggled with the settees. She had inched the china cabinet over towards the fireplace and our family heirlooms sat on the hearthrug, wanting to know what the hell I was going to do about it.

We have an agreement. Aileen has promised never to try and wash up anything with a face value of more than one pound fifty and in return I have promised never to make her feel guilty about it.

The modern mixer tap with its obtrusive spout has a lot to answer for, in our case the maiming of a vast army of innocent teapots, gravy boats, wine-glasses and a Crown Derby figurine by the name of Florence who had never hurt anybody in her life.

We signed the treaty after Florence lost her left arm, her head and, in all probability, her virginity to the mixer tap, and since then the damage has been restricted to the cats' saucers and free mugs from the Shell garage.

It was now twelve hours since Aileen had come home from Mrs Singh's with her trophy and I was absolutely shattered. I placed the sparkling china on the sparkling glass shelves and told Thermal off for sitting on the egg coddler. I laid the tablecloths back in the side-board drawer and told Frink to get the hell out of it.

And then I'd finished. Time for that special cup of tea that would have been a just reward if we hadn't been drinking it all day long.

I took a cup in for Aileen and found her on the phone to her mother. So I sank gratefully into her recliner chair, reclined it and decided to close my eyes for an hour or so until she'd finished.

79

Her mother is Irish and starts every conversation with a run-down on her life as a child on the south coast of Ireland during the Troubles.

Through my torpor and from Aileen's responses it seemed that she had now reached that point where the conversation touches briefly on Eamonn De Valera and his opposition to the 1921 treaty with the hated British government – she must have been at it for around half an hour then. Time for a good long nap before she brought us up to date on the snooker from the Crucible.

And then, out of the blue, she asked a question. It was out of character and it threw Aileen completely. She wasn't used to this and she floundered badly.

'Today? No – nothing much. I just bought a small corner table, that's all.'

CHAPTER SEVEN

I hadn't been able to concentrate all morning. Cliff and Duggie from Brown and Thomas were downstairs, turning our lounge into a proper drawing-room. They were much more than painters, they were artists, and they were proving it by doing their Michelangelo impression on the embossed ceiling and frieze.

It wasn't that they were noisy – you would hardly know they were there, they made their own cups of tea and never bothered us at all.

It's just this blessed work ethic that chips away at me all the time, telling me *I* ought to be down there doing it myself, ought to be able to fit it in somehow.

Logic told me it made more sense for me to do what I did best and let them get on with what they did best – I would make a lousy job of it anyway. But my father's ghost kept digging its bony finger in my chest and shaking its bony head at me.

'*And how much is it costing you?*'

'I can earn more doing this.'

'*If you pulled your finger out, you could do both.*'

* * *

I had no problems when Craig rewired the top two storeys or when Eddie plumbed in the new shower room – I wouldn't have known where to start. But everybody thinks they can paint and hang wallpaper. It's the decorators' curse, and they know very well that everybody can't – they've seen the results.

I am getting better. In restaurants I no longer have to fight the urge to help the waiters.

'Here – let me do that for you. I shall be passing the kitchen on my way to the toilet.'

All the same, I wished I could apply myself and earn that money I was supposed to be earning. Aileen wouldn't be fooling around like this – her concentration had double-glazing fitted as standard.

As though on cue she appeared in the doorway. As always she waited for me to say something, not wanting to break into my train of thought. One day I'm going to drop dead at my desk and it will be a fortnight before she finds out. Well, lunchtime anyway.

'Hello, love.'

'Are you busy?'

I had my feet up on the desk, a glass of red wine in my left hand and a cigarette in my right; but the real giveaway was the small white kitten who was fast asleep and snoring it's head off on the keyboard of my word processor. Of course I could have been sitting there thinking, but she knows I don't do a lot of that.

'I've never stopped all morning.'

I don't know how I would adjust to a wife with normal sight. I have become so used to trotting out these little face-saving lies.

'Is it dusty in here?'

'No. I gave it a wipe round before you got up.'

'Oh – that was nice of you.'

I would earn a Brownie point for that and Aileen would be happy – her dust detector doesn't really work properly until the dust is about a half an inch thick and bounces back when she pokes it.

She came in and plonked herself down on the settee.

'I can't seem to work properly,' she said, 'I've been playing stiffening up with Tigger.'

Stiffening up is a game played between consenting cats and gullible adults. At night Aileen and I will be watching television and the cats will spread themselves at regular intervals all along the hearthrug and the scene will be one of peace and tranquillity.

Then the cats, as one moggie, will swivel their heads sharply, stiffen up and stare in unison at the door. They must have heard something – have they seen anything?

I switch on every light in the hall and then on the stairs, swinging the toffee hammer in my hand and shouting, 'Is there anybody there?' in a deep masculine voice, very loudly so that any intruder will have a sporting chance of being halfway up the M62 before I appear on the scene.

It always seems to happen just as Charlotte Rampling is about to take her clothes off and by the time I return to the television she's got most of them back on again.

There never is anybody there. The cats seem to have a warped sense of humour, but Aileen gets her own back on them.

Tigger sits for hours on the window-sill in Aileen's office, staring out at the side road and the garden path, waiting to bang on the glass if a passing sparrow happens to set as much as one foot on our wall.

Aileen sits beside her, swinging her legs and staring aimlessly out of the window. Then, all of a sudden, she will swivel her head sharply, stiffen up and stare at nothing on the garden path. The cat goes rigid.

'*What?*'

Aileen is locked in a trance, eyes wild and staring.

'*Have you seen something?*'

The cat, now looking as though it has been recently starched, tries desperately to pick out whatever it is she's looking at.

'*Where is it?*'

Aileen packs it in just before the twitch in Tigger's eye is
in danger of becoming a permanent affliction. You would
think it might teach the cats a lesson, but it never does –
it just makes us feel that little bit better.

'Tell you what,' she said. 'Let's give work a rest for a
while.'

Well, I was all in favour of doing that, in fact I had
been practising all morning. I told Frink to keep the
keyboard warm in my absence and we went downstairs
to see how Cliff and Duggie were getting on.

They were bringing the frieze to life, adding just a touch
of colour to the embossed design; a delicate dash of pink
to the occasional flower, the merest hint of green to a
leaf here and there.

It was all very subtle and exactly what we had asked
for, but in the real world subtlety of this sort is lost on
Aileen – it was so subtle she couldn't see it.

'Here – I'll steady the steps while you go up and have
a look.'

She climbed gingerly, step by step. Cliff and Duggie
joined me at the bottom, each of us with a hand on the
stepladder like a support team in a circus.

She stopped at the top, which I thought was very
sensible of her, and trained her trusty binoculars on the
frieze.

We waited, breath bated, for her verdict.

'It's all white.'

Duggie heaved a sigh of relief.

'All *white*,' I explained. 'Aileen, that one hasn't been
painted – it *is* white. Try panning to the left.'

She panned to the left and then to the right.

'I can't see anything.' She lowered the binoculars.
'Couldn't we make them a bit brighter?'

Cliff considered this. 'We could add some darker veins
to the leaves and touch up the tips of the flowers a bit.'

'Would you?'

'No trouble.'

I left them to it and went back to work and maybe I might have achieved something, but it seemed such a shame to disturb the kitten. She was stretched out across the keyboard, practising her breaststroke and doing a little typing on the side. She had stamped seven lines on the computer, each one consisting solely of the letter p.

'That's not bad, Frink – but try varying it a little.'

She didn't answer, just nodded dozily, and another row and a half appeared from nowhere. I moved her chin three-quarters of an inch to the left and very gently lowered it back on the keyboard. A row of nines appeared as if by magic.

'You see, you can do it.'

Do it in her sleep in fact.

An idea had been itching away at the back of my head, a way of appeasing my father's ghost. The ceiling in the old kitchen was a disgrace. The wallpaper had lasted well enough and the revamped cooker positively glowed along one wall. Along another Thermal's litter tray was still in pristine condition and looked even more imposing than the freezer that stood to attention by its side.

Thermal was desperately proud of his litter tray and refused point blank to let any of the other cats use it. Well, it's not nice, is it? Had he been able to flush it, then it might have been a different story – but until science caught up with his feline sensibilities, then whatever it was he found in there he wanted to be absolutely sure that it was one of his own.

It's not nice either when a litter tray looks in better nick than a ceiling, and the more I looked at it the more I was sure that, with my secret weapon, I could have it all done and dusted in no time at all.

I wield a mean roller. Van Gogh couldn't get a better finish on a ceiling. Cliff and Duggie might have the edge on me downstairs when it came to squiggles and fancy bits, but I would defy even Michelangelo to go round a fluorescent strip light as neatly as I can without using a two-inch paint-brush. (If you look carefully, you'll see that they don't have a single fluorescent lighting fitment in the Sistine Chapel. He chickened out.)

The trouble is – I do tend to splatter a lot. I paint the cooker, the carpet and several cats at the same time, and dustsheets solve the problem only until I have to move them along.

Then I can't quite remember which way I had them up in the first place and I tend to sort of potato-print everything I am supposed to be protecting with small spots and enormous great splodges.

So when I saw the man in a television advert merrily rolling away with his pipe stuck in the corner of his mouth and not a dustsheet in sight, I sat up and took notice.

It was apparently such good paint that his sheepdog thought it was cream cheese, but I put that down to the fact that it was probably a very stupid sheepdog. It came not in a tin but in a tray, and down in the cellar I had a two and a half litre block in finest apricot-white waiting for me with its tongue hanging out.

I read the instructions: 'Just draw the roller along the surface, exerting a slightly downward pressure.' I drew the roller towards me and, lo and behold, there it was on my sheepskin ready for slapping on the ceiling.

It would only take me ten minutes and it would be a nice surprise for Aileen. With my unique wrist action I began to attack the job in hand and in no time at all I had half the ceiling done.

Thermal, who usually goes to stay with friends the moment he sees the first dustsheet being lashed into position, strolled into the kitchen, totally unaware that I was poised several feet above his head, and began to inspect his bowl of Whiskas.

He is very careful these days. He once found that he had worked his way into a tin of Cardinal Polish before he realized that it tasted neither of pilchard nor of tuna. Satisfied that this was the real thing, he got stuck into it whilst I slapped away with my roller above his little bowed head.

We were both doing rather well. I had reached the awkward bit where the cornice juts out over the pantry and Thermal had dug down as far as the layer of crunchy biscuit bits I had mixed in with his pilchards to make them more interesting.

I was just wondering if I should have provided him with a hard hat when all of a sudden he heard me and, as he looked up, a big blob of emulsion fell from my roller and caught him slap bang on the nose.

Now for me this was a stroke of luck. Had it not been for Thermal, that blob would now be lying on its back in the middle of the carpet.

Whether Thermal saw it as a stroke of luck is another matter altogether. He went berserk, charging round the kitchen like a cat possessed, the apricot-white blob on his nose giving him a cross-eyed alien look – the kitten from planet X, the kitten that time forgot.

I nipped down the steps and caught him by the draining board as he was about to set out on his third circuit of the kitchen. He seemed quite pleased to be in firm hands until I reached for the dishcloth and began to wipe the emulsion from his nose.

It spread all over his face. He looked like a panda, but I knew I had to get it off before it dried. I carried him over to the sink and scrubbed away at his little nose with just a smidgeon of Ajax liquid and in seconds his face began to foam up.

There was no doubt about it, he did not like it, and he caught me with a well-timed left hook followed by a right cross. He certainly punched his full bodyweight, and as I reeled backwards he slipped and fell into the washing-up bowl.

He launched himself from a submerged dinner plate up on to the draining board and from there he took a mighty leap on to the plank I had suspended between two pairs of steps.

He's a good leaper. He always lands on at least three of his available paws and this time he made it with all four of them – right into the tray of emulsion paint.

He paused but for a moment, and then he took off again along the full length of the plank. Jumping down, he cut across the corner of the kitchen carpet and out into the hall.

I followed him but he was nowhere to be seen. Little apricot-white paw-prints in a serried series of four traced down the hall carpet and out through the back door. I could have followed him – I wouldn't have had to be a Red Indian scout to do that – but I didn't. I had work to do here.

It didn't take as long to clear up as I thought it might. The paint on the kitchen carpet where Thermal had landed from the plank had been thoroughly massaged in, but he must have travelled through the hall at such a speed that the emulsion had been merely stroked against the pile. One wipe with a cloth and it was gone.

The ceiling was a credit to me and I went off in search of Aileen so that I could collect my gold star. I would just mention it in passing.

'Oh by the way – I've painted the kitchen ceiling.'

'You've what?'

'Painted the kitchen ceiling.'

'When?'

'Just now.'

That's the best part. The modest announcement, the delighted reaction. Then she would run upstairs to have a look.

'You've made a good job of it – it looks so much brighter.'

She wouldn't be able to see a thing, of course. In fact I needn't have bothered painting the ceiling at all – I could simply have told her I had and saved all that trouble.

'I think you're wonderful.'

'Yes – I suppose I am really.'

At that point she would stamp on my foot – but first of all I had to find her, then she could tell me how wonderful I was.

I took a detour to see if the postman had called. He had – there was a pile of junk mail lying on the back doormat. I love junk mail because at least I know then that the post has been delivered. We have rotating postmen these days and they come from different directions. One seems to have a round that starts in Great Yarmouth and takes in Portsmouth town centre via an industrial estate just north of Berwick-on-Tweed. The other begins his round outside our coalplace door and is rattling the letterbox a few minutes after midnight.

An empty doormat tells me nothing. I don't know whether they had no post for us today or whether they are yet to come, and so I am running up and down-stairs every five minutes to find out.

A catalogue from Kaleidoscope puts my mind at rest and has the added advantage of making me wonder how I ever lived without an automatic tie rack.

Where was Aileen? Try the lounge, perhaps they were still sorting out the frieze in there. I pushed open the door and my eyeballs screamed and pulled my lids shut from the inside.

One section of the frieze was a mass of living colour. Every little detail had been either touched up or picked out. The man who paints gipsy caravans and canal boats would have been as jealous as hell.

Aileen put her binoculars down as she heard me come in.

'I can see it now,' she cried triumphantly as she picked them up again. And then she frowned as she fiddled with the focus, 'Well almost – what do you think?'

Cliff and Duggie spread their hands to let me know that it wasn't their idea, they were only obeying orders, but any decent court martial would have taken them out and had them shot. I tried to let her down lightly and failed miserably.

'It looks like a greyhound stadium.'

'How do you mean?'

'I don't know. I've never been in a greyhound stadium but I should imagine that's what they look like.'

'You mean it's too much?'

'I mean it's too much – it looked lovely before.'

She sat down on the settee with an air of defeat that normally wouldn't have dared come within yards of her.

'It's so frustrating. It was my idea – but everyone else will be able to enjoy it except me.'

It was one of those problems to which there is no answer. I searched for a platitude, but I seem to have worn out every last one of them over the years. As usual Aileen came to my rescue.

'Does it look really naff?'

'It looks really naff.'

Arthur walked in to have a word with me. Arthur takes being a cat very seriously and from the expression on his face this looked as though it might be rather important. Then he took one look at the frieze and the hairs stood up all along his back and he reversed out into the hall, his mission forgotten for the moment.

'It's frightened Arthur.'

Aileen sighed and then a smile began to muscle in until it had taken over the territory.

'I suppose if we had company – I'd look a bit stupid sitting here with my binoculars.'

'Just a bit.'

She rose to her feet, the decision made.

'Right chaps – thanks for trying. Let's get it back the way it was.'

Duggie and Cliff gratefully dipped their brushes in the white emulsion and began returning the frieze to some sort of sanity. Aileen sank back on the settee.

'Now – I wonder what I could do with that fireplace?'

*   *   *

Thermal came back in time for supper. His paws were wiped clean but his nose had taken on the status of a feature. It was a talking point of a nose and it seemed to walk into the room long before he did.

Later that night, under the guise of an eventide stroke, I filed away at him with one of Aileen's emery boards. He can take any amount of that. He shuts his eyes and holds his nose out to dry and I sort of play him like a violin.

It seemed to be working, but he was going to have to put in many long cat hours himself before he began to look anything like the Thermal we all knew and loved.

He climbed up my chest and hung his head over my shoulder and we had forty winks together – it takes it out of you, this nose filing. I was the first to wake up, and since he had now draped himself around both my shoulders like a fur boa, I was able to study him at the closest of close quarters.

There was something not quite right about him and at first I thought he might have chicken-pox. He was covered all over in tiny white spots. You know how it is – at first you see just the one spot and then . . .

. . . and then there were hundreds of them and they weren't white, they were apricot-white – just like the emulsion. I shuffled Thermal over on to the arm of the chair and hurried out into the kitchen where I began to study the cooker as closely as I had studied the cat.

They were all over the place, the fridge, the microwave, the carpet, all the working surfaces – the whole damn place had been pebble-dashed with apricot-white spots.

I should have known better. There's no such thing as a short cut, and before I went up to bed I must have worn out half a dozen scouring pads and several fingertips.

I wonder if that man in the advert has had a close look at his sheepdog lately – I bet it's got chicken-pox.

*   *   *

The next morning I spent the first hour or so shaving the cooker with a razor blade and then, in the run up to lunchtime, I concentrated my energies on plucking the cat. The cooker took it in its stride, but Thermal was totally bemused by all this attention.

'*Get off.*'

I managed to keep control of the situation until I went to work on his tail.

'*I've warned you.*'

There was a particularly awkward patch on the tip of his tail where several spots had ganged up together to put on a show of strength.

'*Right – that's it.*'

He took a flyer off my knee and bolted out into the hall, looking for Aileen to warn her that I was now heavily into unnatural practices and that perhaps it might be better in future if I were kept well away from the kitten.

I went in search of Aileen – to put my side of the story.

She was downstairs with Duggie and Cliff. They were admiring the fireplace and Aileen called me over as I entered the room.

'Come and look at this.'

She pointed to a small carving just under the mantel-shelf. About a foot across and six inches deep, it featured a jungle of what might be sprawling ivy leaves, reaching out to what might or might not be a leaping salmon at either end.

I had never really taken much notice of it before. Over the years it had been steadily stained along with the rest of the fireplace, until it had become just part-and-parcel of the whole.

But not any more. The ivy had been picked out in the freshest of greens and the salmon in a healthy pink – the fireplace seemed to be smiling at me.

Aileen smiled along with it as she took my hand and led me closer.

'It's my very own personal frieze – I can see this one.'

She picked up her huge Sherlock Holmes magnifying glass and bent over the carving for a moment or so, her brow folded in a frown as she concentrated.

Then she turned and smiled at me again.

'Well – almost.'

CHAPTER EIGHT

T he first few weeks of May had taken out an overdraft with June and blown it all on a large dose of sunshine. The lesser-spotted T-shirts flew in early from the south, and the greater-crested anoraks gathered on the telephone wires before migrating for the season; one or two of the hardier anoraks would take refuge in the shade of the railway station and spend the rest of the summer collecting train numbers.

The waitress in the Leeds coffee shop gave this blast of hot air a typical Yorkshire welcome.

'We'll suffer for this – you just see if we don't.'

I am not on first-name terms with Leeds yet. I can drive straight to the local radio station from home as long as I don't think of anything else on the way there, and if I can find any one of the three bookshops in the town centre, then I can find the other two.

I once found Radio Aire. They were to interview me about my book *Diana's Story* and I was allotted three minutes between records. The presenter waved me to a seat, back announced the previous disc, and then said, 'Tell me – don't you think it's in bad taste, writing a funny book about your first wife's death?'

I was absolutely stunned. I remember mumbling something to the effect that it was not about her death but about her life, and then my three minutes were up and I was being ushered out of the studio.

It has occurred to me since that I might go back and rearrange him so that he wears his earphones on the inside of his head, but I was so shell-shocked on the way home that I would probably never find my way there again.

I seemed to be lost this morning. I knew exactly where my car was – I could see it in my mind's eye, parked outside the florist's shop. If only I could find the florist's shop, or the street, or even the street next to that street.

That was the one where I had thrown the ten-pence piece into the beggar's cap; the one where he had run after me and given it back because he wasn't a beggar and he was only sitting down to take the weight off his feet. If I could find that street then I was sure I could find my car.

I had an idea it might be down there, so I took a short cut through the Marks & Spencer store – twice. The first time I came out the other side with a couple of prawn and mayonnaise sandwiches in a plastic box and the second time I went back in to pay for them.

'I think you've lost one out of here.'
'No it's all right, I've eaten it.'

Sometimes I really do fear for my sanity, but since I wouldn't be able to recognize it if I saw it I can never be absolutely sure whether I've lost it or not.

The problem is my mind is forever leaving me and going off foraging on its own, hanging out with strangers at the first whiff of a good line.

'He's got a wonderful job working with mice – he stretches them.'

He does what? Here, come back! But it's no good – my mind is off running down the street, wanting to hear more, on its own again, with me going round in circles until it decides to return home.

But one good thing about going round in circles is that you find yourself in places you would never have found yourself in if you had gone in a straight line.

And I found myself outside a florist's shop, and right outside the florist's shop, stretched out by the kerb and soaking in the morning sunshine, was my bright red Lancia. I had better get it home before it started to peel.

I slipped my key in the lock but it wouldn't turn. It did that sometimes, so I walked round to the passenger door and tried it there. That's funny, this one wouldn't work either. The car liked to have a game with me now and again but it had never taken it this far before, it usually knew when to stop.

The window was wound down a couple of inches. Perhaps I could get my arm inside. But then, as I slipped my hand over the glass, the woman sitting in the passenger seat wound it up again and I nearly lost four fingers in one go.

She sat very still and stared resolutely out through the windscreen. I bent down and stared in her left ear. What was she doing there? I banged on the glass but the ear took no notice and then a man arrived at the driver's door and placed a box containing a dozen or so bedding plants on my roof.

'What are you playing at?' he wanted to know.

'What am *I* playing at? I think it's . . .'

I didn't go any further. This car had a baby's safety-seat in the back – mine didn't. It had a purple monkey with an orange bottom swinging on the rear-view mirror – mine didn't. This car was clean – mine hadn't been washed for months (it weakens them). Oh my God! It was the hub-caps all over again.

'I'm sorry – I think I've got the wrong car.'

'I think you have – now shove off.'

Well, I couldn't leave it at that. That's always been my trouble – I never could leave it at that.

'I've got the same car myself,' I told him. 'It's the same

model, the same colour and I'm sure I parked it here. You don't see many Lancias – I just never thought.'

He cast his eyes up the street and then he cast his eyes down the street.

'Where is it then?'

I wished I could have told him – I couldn't see it either.

'I'm sure I parked it here.'

'Oh aye?' He was even more suspicious of me now than he had been when he caught me making faces at his wife through the window.

There were only two cars in the entire street. This one and a racy white number butted up to its rear bumper.

'Maybe I parked it in the next street.'

But I was sure I hadn't. The only thing I was sure of now was that I had it with me when I drove into Leeds.

I bent down again to apologize to the wife, but the husband growled so I thought perhaps that might not be a very good idea. So I disappeared up a sidestreet to find and beat the living daylights out of my Lancia for not being where it ought to be.

I combed every street within spitting distance and very slowly the idea began to dawn on me that it might have been stolen. It had never occurred to me before. I mean, who would want to steal a car that looked as though it hadn't the energy to start, never mind move.

I had completed a second circuit and was just about to phone the police when I saw it. It looked so beautiful that I ran down the street and across the pavement with my arms wide open to give it a big kiss.

Then I saw the box of bedding plants on the roof and I skidded to a halt, dug my hands deep in my pockets and began to whistle a selection of Elkie Brooks's greatest hits as I strolled past four extremely suspicious eyes and a purple monkey with an orange bottom.

The eyes were still burning a hole in the back of my head when my mind came trotting along the pavement towards me as though it hadn't a care in the world. I stood with arms folded, ready to give it a piece of itself.

'Where the hell have you been?'

'*Never mind that – let's get going.*'

'And how are we going to do that?'

'*Get in the car and I'll tell you.*'

It nodded to the white racy number, the one that had been lazing in the sunshine behind the Lancia. It was a Subaru XT Turbo and it had too much class to get involved in sordid squabbles.

'*Don't you remember? You bought it last week, when you sold the Lancia.*'

'Of course.'

I tugged the keys from my pocket, jabbed them in the lock and slid gratefully behind the steering wheel. My mind slumped beside me in the passenger seat.

'How could I have forgotten?'

'*You're not fit to be let loose on your own.*'

'You shouldn't just bugger off and leave me like that.'

'*I needed the exercise – I don't get very much with you.*'

Through the rear window of the Lancia in front I could see a pair of heads staring at me as though they were on the wrong way round. What was it I had told them? 'I've got the same car myself – it's the same colour, the same model and I'm sure I parked it here.'

And now here I was, sitting in a white one right behind them. I'd better go and explain.

'*I shouldn't if I were you.*'

'They'll understand – it could happen to anyone. Are you coming?'

'*No – I think I'll stay here.*'

I climbed out of the car and walked towards them, but they couldn't have seen me coming. The man fired his engine and the Lancia took off like a rocket. I stepped out in the road and picked up his tray of bedding plants from where they had fallen off the roof.

98

I waited for over an hour for them to come back, but they never did. It wasn't an inconvenience – I had to wait for the mechanic to come and start the car for me.

He was very pleasant. I thought it might have been my fault but he said no, it was just a case of loose wiring.

He got in the car to fill in the appropriate forms and apologized profusely for sitting on my bedding plants. 'I'll pay for them,' he said. I told him not to bother. 'No, I'll pay for them – they're not cheap these days.'

I argued, but he insisted on knocking a couple of pounds off the bill and I suggested that since he'd paid for them he might as well have what was left of them, but apparently he'd only just moved into a flat and they would have been wasted.

My new car simply purred along the M62 and I just couldn't understand how I could have forgotten about it. I was in love with the thing.

'It's just that I'm absent-minded.'

'Don't drag me into it.'

A green light appears when the turbocharger comes into play. A police car waited patiently on his little lump by the side of the motorway. The light went off again – quick.

'I could use it in the book.'

'Use what?'

'That business with the Lancia.'

'They'll think you're an idiot.'

'No they won't. They'll think I'm lovable – absent-minded, but lovable.'

'As long as you let them know that I wasn't there.'

The police car had tucked itself in behind me and I was having the devil's own job keeping the car under seventy. The speedometer seemed to have been greased.

'Do you fancy a cup of coffee?'

'Be very nice.'

I pulled off the motorway and slipped up the slip road towards the Hartshead Service Station. The police car carried on towards Huddersfield.

'Do you mind if I mention something?'
'No.'
'You won't get mad?'
'No, of course not.'
'Only – you've started talking to yourself again.'

Aileen had a list of messages for me. She carries them in her head and has to reel them off before she becomes sidetracked by small talk.

'. . . and Jim rang – he said he wasn't putting any pressure on you.'

Jim Cochrane is my editor and he puts pressure on me by telling me he wouldn't dream of putting pressure on me.

'I'll ring him in a bit.'

He would be perfectly understanding. He would know how it was and he would tell me I mustn't worry about deadlines or anything like that. The important thing was to get it right. He understood and he would be the last person to put pressure on me.

And then I would put the phone down with guilt dripping out of every pore and I would have made promises I would have to sweat blood to keep.

'I'll put these bedding plants in and then I'll ring him.'

Aileen followed me out into the garden and parked herself on one of the railway sleepers.

'What bedding plants?'

'I bought some bedding plants – there, in that box.'

She turned and caught it with her foot, then leaned over and peered down at the mass of foliage.

'That's wonderful – how many are there?'

'Do you mean altogether?'

'Yes.'

'Three.'

'Three? You only bought three?'

'I didn't really buy them.'

'What did they do – fall off the back of a lorry?'

'Something like that.'

We can't have a minute alone in the garden. First Tigger inched her way under the hedge and came to sit by Aileen. Then Thermal squeezed himself through the bars of the wrought-iron gate and came over to sit by Tigger. I cleared a small area of forest bark and then dug a hole for the first plant.
'You see where he's digging, Tigger.'
'Yes.'
'I had a wee there yesterday morning.'
'Yes I know.'
'How do you know?'
'We all have.'

Somewhere in the back lane a dog worked himself into a frenzy and then Frink the kitten arrived over the wall at breakneck speed. She flopped down breathless for a moment or so on the warm pavers and then came over and perched herself on the sleeper with the others.
'I had a wee there yesterday.'
'We know.'

I found a fourth plant that had narrowly survived the trial-by-mechanic's bottom. It was having trouble with its breathing, but it seemed a plucky little fellow and it deserved its day in the sun.

As I looked around for a likely home for it I noticed Arthur sitting patiently on the other side of the gate. He was too fat to squeeze between the bars, and the alternative route involved the scaling of two drystone walls and a death-defying abseil down the other side. I mentioned it to Aileen and she went over and held the gate open for him.

Arthur still has trouble dealing with the normal courtesies in life – he just isn't used to them. He is a very polite little chap in himself, but his experience of human beings before he came to live with us seems to have been limited to those with short tempers and steel toecaps.

He sat where he was for a while – it could be a trap, you can't be too sure. He'd walked into more traps than he'd had hot dinners and it could be a very painful business.

His brain takes a considerable time to warm up, and long before the first glow appeared on the horizon Aileen had already shut the gate and was back on the sleeper with the other three. She looked around for Arthur.

'Where's he gone?'

'He hasn't even been – he's still making his mind up.'

She tried again, this time waiting until the faint glow heated itself up to gas-mark six. He had a good stretch and then waddled in to see what was going on. He nodded to Aileen in passing.

'Thank you very much.'

'My pleasure, Arthur.'

The earth was dry and the hole delighted in refilling itself. I tossed the trowel aside and held the landslide back with my hand. Frink came closer to inspect the situation for herself.

'That's where I had a wee, Arthur.'

Arthur snorted and thrust his back leg in the air.

'That's nothing to what I did.'

It was very pleasant out there in the garden and now that I had self-started I might as well do a little light weeding. The others left me to it and went about their business. Aileen would have given me a hand, but when it comes to weeding she's never quite sure what to pull out and what to leave alone.

The forest bark stopped at the wrought-iron gate and without its woody presence the weeds on the other side were running amok. There was a gang of them over there, mugging a small wallflower.

'Don't worry – I'm coming.'

Without a thought for my own safety I was in amongst them and the look on the wallflower's face was reward enough in itself. I ripped out those whose legs just skim across the surface and then whipped out my trusty trowel to deal with those whose feet were firmly planted in the rich earth.

Within minutes the colour was coming back to the wallflower's cheeks and only the ringleader had any fight left in him. It was him or me.

He was firmly entrenched between a rock and a hard place and I grabbed him by the scruff of the neck. He braced himself against the rock as I dug my trowel down towards his boots and the neighbouring weeds screamed in terror.

It has to be all or nothing with weeds – half measures don't work. I slid my hand down beneath the soil to take stock of his horny roots and at that very moment he produced his secret weapon.

Oh God, I hate slugs. It wasn't the biggest slug I'd ever seen, but that didn't really matter – I'd touched him and it was enough to scar me for life.

I compromised with the weed. I cut him off at the knees and left him to regroup and perhaps to fight another day. The slug I despatched to his maker, although whoever has the gall to make them, I can't for the life of me imagine.

All of a sudden weeding lost its appeal for me. It was rather like fox-hunting – a bit of fun as long as they don't start fighting back. I slipped my trowel into its holster and turned towards the gate. The other wallflowers looked up at me pleadingly and I told them that I would go and fetch help.

If I used the back door for the rest of the summer I wouldn't have to face them again.

I washed my hands and climbed the stairs to my office. An idea was taking shape and I wanted to work it through before I rang Jim Cochrane.

When I lived in Matlock we had slugs like the Pied Piper had mice and they made our life a misery – I could do one of my famous flashbacks, no-one would notice.

And then I remembered writing about them in another book – which one was it? I thumbed through the bookshelf and then stopped at page 104 of *Lost For Words*.

I wondered what had happened to the slugs. I had imagined them, over the winter, entombed in tiny blocks of ice wondering what the hell had hit them. I didn't care what the RSPCA thought – I hoped they had chilblains, frostbite and chapped lips and it damned well served them right.

And that was that. No more than a mention. Right – this is what we do. I would admit to the readers that I had used the passage before, tell them exactly where it came from and quote it in italics. Then carry on. You can get away with murder – all you need is a little bit of cheek.

MAY

But they did survive, and as the spring began to slide into summer they were back again. Whether they hired a coach and nipped off to sunnier climes for the winter, or whether they discovered the delights of the thermal vest I shall never know, but Sally spotted the first one of the season.

'Do me a favour, Dad,' she said. 'There's a dead mouse by the side of the water butt. Nip out and pop it in the dustbin.'

Well, I knew it couldn't be a mouse – the slugs had frightened them off last summer – but I did as I was told and right there on the patio was the biggest slug I had ever seen in my life.

It was huge and black and it moved like a John Player racing car. It turned to face me, a sadistic smile playing round the corners of its mouth, and it was then that I recognized him.

His name was Arnold and he was a troublemaker. I remembered him from the way he dragged his back leg, an old war wound from the time I hit him with a slug pellet. He was one of my rare successes – I'm a lousy shot with a slug pellet and usually I miss.

Out of the corner of my eye I could see a half a dozen

other slugs behind the water butt. They were doing press-ups and pumping iron, making sure they were in peak condition now that the bedding plants were in.

Down by the side of the garage I had a lovely little flower bed. It was only six inches wide but it ran the entire length of the garage and it was a mass of colour – well, not colour exactly. It was a mass of green, it would be a mass of colour when the salvias came out – all five of them.

I wouldn't have minded, but I planted twenty-four of the damned things. I know what happened to six of them. I beheaded five of the poor devils within minutes of planting them because I forgot that the side door opened outwards, and then I ran over the other one with the wheelbarrow.

That left me with eighteen and now I had only the five left. The remaining thirteen proved a rich source of protein for Arnold and his merry band of molluscs.

I couldn't understand how they were getting at them. I had piled slug pellets to a height of three inches around each of the plants, and yet in the morning my salvia leaves would look like trellis work.

At first I thought that the slugs had imported a pole-vaulting slug who was hurling himself over the barrier. Sally suggested that perhaps we had a very rare strain of balancing slugs who were standing on one another's shoulders. But at last we discovered their secret.

They had a specially-trained squad of Kamikaze slugs who were sent in as soon as I drew the kitchen curtains for the night.

They moved in swiftly and silently, three to a plant, and with total disregard for their own safety they either gorged themselves until they had made a sizeable hole in the barrier, or lay on top of the pellets so that their mates could crawl over their twitching bodies. You have to admire them.

All this had come to light after I had cross-examined a young rookie slug I had taken prisoner on a shovel and locked in the stockade – or, as we sometimes called it, the coalplace.

I left him alone for most of the day without food or water – it's what they call psychology and they used it a lot in those old films about Japanese prisoner-of-war camps.

I refused him any mail or Red Cross parcels and I poured water from one glass to another, just outside the door, so that he would get really thirsty.

After ten hours I burst in. Then, waving my toffee hammer and shining a light in his eyes, I shouted, 'OK, sonny – talk.'

His lips were parched and he tried to pretend it didn't hurt him when he smiled. He went white when I threatened him with the toffee hammer but all he would give me was his name, rank and serial number. His name was Ralph and he was a bombardier with the Third Salvia Platoon. I can't remember his serial number.

I wanted him to tell me where his mates hid up during the daytime but he just muttered something about the Geneva Convention, and then he made a break for it.

Sally shouted, 'Hit him with the toffee hammer.'

I said, 'I can't – they go all horrible when you hit them.'

'Just stun him then,' she yelled.

Well – I mean, how do you stun a slug? I looked round and he'd gone.

But it was only as Arnold lay on the paving stones looking like a particularly muscular hamster that I realized just why my garden had become a Mecca for every slug within miles.

Arnold was the equivalent of the Queen Bee – wherever Arnold went his subjects must follow. I scooped him up with the shovel. It wasn't easy, he must have weighed a pound and a half.

I thought, 'If I flip him over the fence into next-door's garden, all his mates will go and join him.' And so, whirling the shovel around my head, I projected him into space.

Or so I thought. When I looked down at the shovel, there was Arnold clinging on for dear life. He saw me watching him and he curled his lip and sneered once more.

I banged the shovel on the fence and I hammered it against the apple tree. It was like trying to get rid of chewing gum. I could almost hear him singing, 'We shall not be moved.'

I thought, *To hell with this*, and I let go of the shovel and it flew over the fence with Arnold acting as a test pilot, still clinging on grimly. *A good day's work*, I thought, and went in to pour myself a stiff whisky.

I was standing by the window, fondly contemplating a slug-free summer, when the shovel came hurtling back over the fence. It made a three-point landing, veered slightly to the right, and shuddered to a halt just to the left of the water butt.

After an interval of a few seconds Arnold undid his safety harness, adjusted his helmet and goggles and, dragging his bad leg behind him, made for his mates, who were now waving their scarves and singing something that sounded suspiciously like, 'You'll never walk alone.'

I collapsed into a chair and poured myself another drink. Not only had I lost the battle – I'd lost the bloody war as well.

I read the piece aloud to Aileen. She sat on the low stool and listened with her chin cupped in her hands.

'What do you think?'

She hesitated for a moment or so, then took a cigarette from her packet and pulled the stool a little closer.

'It's a bit fanciful, isn't it?'

'It's supposed to be fanciful.'

'Slugs don't have legs.'

'They don't wave scarves or sing, "You'll Never Walk Alone" either – it's supposed to be fanciful.'

She pulled hard on her cigarette, so I leaned over and lit it for her.

'A bombardier with the Third Salvia Platoon?'

'It's just make-believe.'

'It's just another flashback – and it's got nothing to do with Huddersfield.'

I thought about that for a moment.

'I'm going to do a piece about mixing up the cars this morning.'

'That was in Leeds.'

'It's not far away.'

'And there's no protein in a salvia.'

'Look,' I said. It was make-your-mind-up time. 'What do you really think?'

'What do you want me to say?'

'I want you to say that it's very funny and you think it's brilliant.'

'All right. It's very funny and I think it's brilliant.'

'Good.'

I fed twenty sheets of paper into the printer and went off to ring Jim. I could tell him that I had started writing again and that Aileen loved it. And she wouldn't say so if she didn't mean it – would she?

CHAPTER NINE

Thermal had just got himself settled when the phone rang and he didn't want to know about it. He'd done things right, he'd gone through the proper rituals – the compulsory five-minute pound on my lap, followed by the statutory shuffling of the bottom, and all he asked now were a few more minutes to enjoy the fruits of his labour. And then the bloody phone goes and rings – life could be very unfair.

'*Ignore it.*'

The phone gave a third ring, followed by a stifled yelp as it was cut off in mid trill.

'I can't – it's your mum, she wants picking up.'

Aileen also has her rituals. Once a week I drop her off outside the Sue Ryder charity shop in Marsh where she spends a happy half hour sifting and sorting through the dross and the desirable.

Last October she strolled into the Women of the Year Luncheon at the Savoy Hotel wearing a £500 suit by Parigi and a £1.50 shirt from the Sue Ryder charity shop in Marsh. The Duchess of Kent said she liked her blouse ever so much, and Aileen said she would see if she could find her one just like it. She never has, but it's not for the lack of trying.

Then it's across the road to Trudy's to have her hair done. Out comes the telescopic white stick – she can always find that, it's in her handbag, but that beep-button on the traffic lights can be an elusive little devil. Not that it usually matters.

'Come on, love.'

An anonymous hand takes hold of her elbow and whisks her across the road, parting the four lanes of traffic like Moses on one of his better days.

'Thank you ever so much.'

'Don't mention it.'

Now then, let's see. Trudy's isn't quite opposite the lights – it's one shop down. Went into the electrical shop last week by mistake, they were very nice – I must go in there after I have had my hair done and have another look at that kettle. Better hurry now or someone will have me back across the road.

A blonde leans out of the hairdresser's door. She looks up and down the road, then shakes her head. I don't know – where can she be? She's late again. Ah, there she is.

'Come on with you.'

They discuss her hair. Aileen tells Trudy how she wants it and Trudy tells Aileen how she's going to get it and two hours later my phone rings three times. Then I have to peel this velcroed cat from my knee and go searching for her.

I never know where she is – she could be anywhere in Marsh by this time. Often she's on the pavement outside Mrs Singh's second-hand emporium, half hidden in a graveyard of refrigerators. But not today – perhaps she's gone inside?

I stand on the edge of the pavement and stare across the road. Mrs Singh must be away this morning because

Big John is in charge and he stands in the doorway watching Colin and Steve as they grunt and dump a four-seater settee outside the window.

Little John sits dreaming in a winged easy by the ornamental chimney pots, letting the others get on with it. It's good to see him back at work again. A car hit him as he was crossing the road a month or so ago, but his leg is out of plaster now and he will be able to start mapping out his colourful social life once more.

Great chunks of his working day seem to be spent in the planning of his flamboyant nights and even now he seems lost to the world as he runs delicate fingers through his fair hair.

He's probably wondering if he could get away with that little red dress this evening, the one with no back and the sequins, and if so, what shoes he should wear with it. I don't know – it's decisions, decisions. He shakes his head as he catches sight of me and gives me a wave of his hand.

'She's not here.'

He's lost a lot of weight since that car ran over him – he looks just like a wrist on a stick.

She could have popped in to Marsh Carpets, of course. She's been after another Chinese rug for ages. I think she wants a matching pair so she can breed from them.

Mike and Jean shake their heads in unison as I pass by the window. I wonder where she is?

She might have gone on to the Midland Bank. We have our own small branch in Marsh. It's like a rabbit hutch with central heating and it's my favourite bank in the whole wide world. I've got to pop in anyway, to hand over a cheque for my income tax.

She isn't there and the fact doesn't take much establishing. If they have half a dozen customers in the bank at any one time then it's absolutely packed – seven, and you're writing on somebody else's cheque stub.

Behind the counter Karen glances at the amount I have donated to the Inland Revenue and winces.

'Oh, love – I am sorry.'

You can see why I like it. In the main branch, down in Cloth Hall Street, we have a row of machines that are invaluable on a Sunday morning; but here in Marsh, the Midland is the Wincing Bank.

There's quite a queue in the post office across the road, it winds itself twice around the birthday cards. The woman at the front is holding everything up while the staff explain to her that there is no point in stockpiling first-class stamps in case they go up.

They are very polite and patient with her. I would have hit her with my date stamp before now. She goes off on a different tack.

'Can you tell me – is Jersey abroad?'

Behind the counter Thelma takes a firm grip on her date stamp and then shakes her head and gives me a big smile as she sees me inspecting the queue.

'She's not been in here.'

They really are very nice people, and yet I have bought thousands of stamps from them since I arrived in Huddersfield and not once have they offered to knock a penny off for me in discount. I couldn't do it myself. Still, I suppose either you have a generous nature or you haven't.

Outside the Marsh House a couple are drinking at a white plastic table. They seem to be going through a difficult time and are each blaming the other for it, screaming at one another with their noses not an inch apart.

As he walks past, a policeman suddenly becomes very interested in the dry cleaners across the road – doesn't want to know about this, it's a domestic, you see.

Isn't it strange how civilization has conditioned us? If they had been making love he would have arrested them.

On past the cake shop and a lady I just can't place smiles at me and points down the road.

'She's in Graham's.'

'Right, thank you.'

She must be buying the fruit and vegetables for the week. If I walk slowly she'll have paid for them by the time I get there. A lady I have never seen before in my life shouts from across the other side of Westbourne Road.

'She's in Graham's.'

'Thank you very much.'

Might as well try Graham's – it's a long shot, but you never know.

Trudy bangs on the window as I pass by, pointing next door with a pair of scissors and mouthing: 'She's in Graham's.'

She should know – Graham is her husband.

She wasn't in Graham's. She had been, but she wasn't there now.

'She left this for you.'

Graham pointed to one of his special carrier bags, packed to the gunnels with fruit and veg. The bags had been on offer so he'd bought the lot. They were about the size of a dustbin liner with two handles at the top, and it was a common sight around here to see old-age pensioners dragging them out of his shop and across the pedestrian crossing. The regulation height for an old-age pensioner in Huddersfield is five foot four and they couldn't handle them.

'I shall be glad when you've got rid of these.'

'What's wrong with them?'

'They stretch – they get even longer by the time you get them home.'

'Never mind, there's only a couple of thousand left.'

I slung it over my shoulder and staggered towards the door.

'Have you any idea where Aileen's got to?'

'She's next door – in Roy's.'

'Right, thank you.'

'Don't mention it – that will be £12.95 if you don't mind.'

She wasn't in Roy's. She had been, but she wasn't there now.

'She left these for you.'

Roy handed a couple of carrier bags over the counter. At least they were your average, honest-to-goodness sort of carrier bags that get on with the job and don't make a fuss about it – not like the one that was now mutating round my neck and over my shoulder. It had grown another foot already and I hadn't travelled more than a dozen yards – I had to use both hands to keep it off the floor.

'What have we got in here?'

'Pork and beef, half a dozen sausages, and she bought a meat and potato pie for Zak.'

'Right.'

'So that's £15.39.'

The lady standing next to me was very good. She tugged my wallet out of my back pocket and paid him for me. Then she slid it back in – it was the highlight of my day so far.

'Have you lost her again?'

'Yes. Do you know where she is?'

'She was in the chemist's not a couple of minutes ago.'

I held the door open with one foot and juggled with the carrier bags. Graham's was now about five foot long and it was undulating, like a snake who had just swallowed a baby buffalo – you could see the outline of the carcass as it was slowly being digested.

There seemed to be quite a lot of room in the top now, so I dropped the new bags inside the old one and tried to ignore the muffled screams as they slipped down its throat.

Zak was waiting for me outside. He'd just mugged some poor soul in the bus queue and was eating a packet of crisps. He spat out the packet and came over.

He isn't the prettiest dog in Huddersfield, but then boxers always have had a world-weary look about them. Zak is the original hangdog – he's an expert on melancholia. He has perfected the fine art of being miserable and turned it into a science.

Do you remember Geoffrey Palmer as the husband in *Butterflies*? If he goes on the way he is, in thirty years' time he'll look just like Zak.

'Aileen gave you a meat and potato pie – you're not having anything else.'

He spends most of his days outside the butcher's shop and he has few natural enemies. Only Graham next door, who once caught him peeing on his cabbages, would wish him elsewhere; which is why he has now stationed Sheila outside his shop with a bucket of bleach, just in case.

Otherwise all is sweetness and light. Grown men, who would deny their own whippet an extra biscuit at bedtime, dip into their paper bags and hand over a cooked chicken leg to Zak.

He's the butcher's best customer. Roy reckons he gets through seven or eight meat pies a day, plus the odd meat and potato from customers who have difficulty telling them apart.

And not one of these customers ever gets so much as a nod, never mind a thank you; and an appreciative smile would be asking far too much – by the time a smile had rolled back the many folds of that lugubrious face it would have worn itself out and be considering early retirement.

The sadness in those beggar's eyes has always been there, it's in his genes, but the light was turned down another notch at Christmas when his master died and life will never be the same again for Zak. They were very close, and a few meat pies only serve to help the day along.

I dug my hand in the carrier bag and tried to break off a sausage at the elbow for him. But they stick together, these sausages – they link arms and dig their heels in.

No matter how I tugged and twisted, the little devils hung on to one another until, finally, the one at the end could take it no longer. It burst, and my hand shot along its length and came up out of the bag full of sausage meat.

'Here you are, Zak.'

That wasn't my voice. It was the voice of the lady who was now feeding a meat pie to the boxer at my feet. I waited while he finished it – there wasn't really anywhere I could go with a hand full of sausage meat – and he seemed to take for ever. It had been a good day and the meat pies were probably stacked up in his stomach like charter flights over Gatwick.

'Come on – get it down you.'

He stretched and then, pausing only to lick the odd crumb of pastry from the pavement, turned and walked off in the direction of Mrs Singh's.

'Zak.'

He disappeared round the corner by the chemist's and I looked round for a litter-bin. A busy little dog of indeterminate parentage bounced along the pavement towards me, a preoccupied look in his eye as he tried to stick to what seemed to be a pretty rigorous schedule. He was probably a self-made dog who had worked his way up and had his own business, he might be in the market for fast food. I bent down, ready to intercept him.

'Hello, boy – would you like a snack?'

Without breaking step he took in the carrier bag that might well have contained all my worldly possessions and then he saw the outstretched hand.

'*Sorry – I don't carry money on me.*'

And with that he was off, leaving me crouching on the pavement like some geriatric bag lady.

There was a dustbin on the other side of the chemist's wall. They hid it there so that the general public wouldn't toss great dollops of sausage meat in it, but we all knew where it was and found it extremely handy.

I heaved the carrier bag off my shoulder and folded it over the wall, half this side and half that, and then I leaned over and removed the lid from the dustbin.

The dustbin growled, and a rasping tongue that hadn't been shaved in weeks wrapped itself round the sausage meat and it was gone.

'Hello, Zak – I didn't see you there.'

He was too busy to indulge in idle conversation, crouching there in the long grass by the dustbin – his ruckled face looking as though he'd got it on upside down as he strained at his ablutions.

Very handy, this little spot. He could have a crap in private here and it couldn't be more convenient for his day job at the butcher's. And now his meals were even being delivered – it almost made life worth living after all.

She wasn't in the chemist's. She had been, but she wasn't there now.

'She left this for you.'

Chris Holt handed over a bottle of his dreaded Metcolt Adult Cough Remedy. He makes it himself in the back of the shop and Aileen swears by it.

I swear *at* it, and I groaned when I saw the bottle.

'Is this that creosote stuff?'

'No – it's that *purified* creosote stuff.'

There's no doubt about it – it works wonders. There isn't a cough in Christendom that wouldn't bolt in terror if it saw this stuff coming down your throat, but I can't handle it. My hand shakes as I grip the spoon, my eyes water and the muscles in my throat go on strike.

'We've had a meeting and we've decided we'd rather have the cough, if you don't mind. It's quite a nice cough really – once you get used to it.'

I force it down eventually and after a quarter of a pound of mint humbugs, a glass of Jack Daniels sipping whisky and a good roll on the sheepskin rug I feel like a new man.

It also has a built-in bonus. After a couple of doses the cough gives up and goes home to live with its mother and you can creosote the shed with the rest of the bottle.

'That'll be £4.95.'

'Has it gone up?'

'No – there's a lipstick in there as well.'

The carrier bag laid its head on my shoulder and glowered at him. It had twisted itself round my back and its tail hung down by my right leg.

'Have you bought yourself a rug?'

'No – it's one of Graham's carrier bags.'

'They're getting longer, aren't they? I don't usually allow them in here. I make customers chain them to the railings outside.'

I looked for somewhere to put it down while I dipped into my pocket. I needed a long uninterrupted stretch of carpet, out of harm's way, where it wouldn't snap at anyone's ankles. I started laying down its tail by the hairnets and then fed it, yard by yard, past the deodorants and the fast-tanning creams until I had the head tucked out of harm's way by the cotton-wool balls.

'Did Aileen say where she was going?'

Chris might have told me if the man with the limp hadn't stumped in through the door at that point. It was one hell of a limp, it had a personality all of its own and it rolled up to the counter like a camshaft on its day off. Its owner asked for something and Chris handed it to him.

'That'll be £1.95, please.'

The man dug deep into his trouser pocket and came out with a huge fistful of assorted coins. He sifted through them until he found two one-pound pieces.

Chris always tries to be helpful – he doesn't often manage it, but he tries.

'Hang on a minute – let's have a look.'

The man held out his hand and Chris sorted through the coins, ten pence here, five pence there, twenty pence in two-pence pieces, fifteen pence in pennies. He laid them out on the counter.

'There you are – £1.95.'

He handed the two pounds back to the man.

'You might even find your limp's gone now.'

The man dropped the coins into his pocket and picked up his paper bag.

'I don't think so – I've had it ever since I had my leg off.'

The other customers watched as he put the limp into gear and manhandled it out of the shop. I didn't – I was watching Chris's face.

On those days when I have done something particularly stupid I think of Chris. He makes me feel normal.

I stood on the steps, working out my next move. Over at Mrs Singh's, Steve and Colin were wondering how best to display a steel filing cabinet. They stood it on the pavement alongside a child's wooden desk, kicked a wastepaper basket underneath and then stood back to admire their handiwork.

A dirty laugh I would have recognized anywhere came from over by the armchairs. Slinging the carrier bag over my shoulders as once I had seen a farmer carry a small calf, I wandered over to have a word with its owner.

Aileen was deep in conversation with Little John. If she were him, she said, she would go for broke and wear the strapless gold lamé and the slingbacks – in for a penny, in for a pound, that was her motto.

It seemed a shame to disturb them, so I waited until they had sorted out both the earrings and the elbow-length gloves before I prised her away.

On the way home we crossed over the road and walked along the edge of the park. It would have been quite pleasant if I had thought to bring a lead for the carrier bag. It could have had a run and given me a rest.

'I bought an ornamental chimney pot from Mrs Singh's – it will look nice in the garden.'

'Right – I'll fetch it later.'

The carrier bag drooled and licked its lips in anticipation. I tapped it on the nose.

'Down, boy – down.'

'You are talking to yourself again – it's getting to be a habit, you know.'

'I wasn't – I was talking to the carrier bag.'

'Oh I'm sorry,' she said, 'I didn't realize.'

Just before six o'clock that evening the phone rang again and this time it was a relief to hear it. My study had been like a freeway all afternoon with first Aileen putting her head round the door.

'What did you mean – you were talking to the carrier bag?'

And then the cats, in an obviously pre-planned manoeuvre, came in one by one to remind me that it was National Pet Week this week and what the hell was I going to do about it?

I hadn't forgotten. After all, National Pet Week only comes around once a year and you have to make an effort. I was having Arthur and Frink neutered in the morning, but I didn't want to tell them yet – it might spoil the surprise.

At least the phone call could be termed business, if only in the loosest sense. The girl on the other end sported a man's name, she was a Reggie or Charlie or something like that, and she worked for a national magazine.

'We are running a special feature in October, a sort of a day in the life of a writer, or rather several writers – that kind of thing. Could we send someone to see you?'

'Yes – fine.'

'Perhaps you could give me some idea – you know, just a taster of a typical day.'

I suppose I was just lucky that I had had such an eventful morning – usually my life is rather boring and I would have been hard pushed to make anything of it. With the best will in the world, staring into space and tapping at a keyboard can't be said to be the most riveting of pursuits.

'Well, this morning Aileen went to have her hair done . . .'

I told her all about Zak and about Graham's carrier bags, and about the man with a limp and how Little John had eventually decided on the gold lamé and the slingbacks.

She was absolutely fascinated and listened in total silence until I drew to a close some twenty minutes later. I don't suppose it's very often that good stories like that fall straight into her lap.

As a fail-safe I told her that I was having the cats neutered in the morning and if she liked we could tinker with the timing and pretend it had happened today.

She said she would call back and make the final arrangements — but so far I haven't heard a word from her. Perhaps I should give her a ring.

CHAPTER TEN

I seemed to spend the greater part of June in recording studios, first buried deep in the cellars of Soho for the American audio version of *The Cat Who Came In From The Cold*.

From there I moved out to yet another cellar, just off the Finchley Road, where the delightful Mellie Buse steered me through the unabridged version of *Lost For Words*.

I worried in case the Americans might have trouble coming to terms with my English accent, but the powers that be in New York had no doubts whatsoever.

'It'll be fine. We're used to English accents – don't forget we have Alistair Cooke over here.'

So that was all right then. If they could cope with Alistair Cooke and his thick northern vowels, then they could certainly cope with mine.

The first few days in London always disturb me – I feel as though I am a country bumpkin with straw in my hair. The traffic confuses me, the people infuriate me and I can't remember where anywhere is any more.

I make the mistake of talking to people on the underground and then kick myself as the other passengers cringe in embarrassment. It's just not done.

But within twenty-four hours I have thrown away my *A to Z*, I am recommending a restaurant in Covent Garden to an Australian couple and I'm cringing along with my fellow travellers as some country bumpkin attempts to start a conversation on the underground.

I always stay at the Royal Overseas League in St James's. There I do know where everything is from day one and, more importantly, so does Aileen when she is down in London. It's like a second home.

At dinner on the first night I was joined by a well-upholstered lady whose accent was so far back, the Queen Mother would have had trouble understanding her. After a short skirmish with a waiter, she turned to me.

'You must be from the north.'

'Yes – that's right. Yorkshire.'

She laid her bust across three forks and a steak knife as she leaned over towards me and asked confidentially, as though I might be ashamed if the others found out, 'Tell me – what is it *really* like up there?'

As usual I tried to sell it to her. For some reason I always go on about the Lake District and how beautiful it is, even though I've only ever seen it twice myself and on both occasions it was chucking it down with rain. I threw in the Derbyshire Dales and the Yorkshire Moors for good measure and then began to feel rather ashamed of this pitiful attempt to justify my existence.

'. . . anyway, at least we've stopped binding the children's feet.'

At first she seemed pleased about that, but then she had second thoughts and wagged her finger at me, giving me a look that told me she wasn't born yesterday.

'You mustn't pull my leg, young man – they haven't done that sort of thing since the war, have they?'

But as soon as I take my seat on the Yorkshire Pullman

and head back north, my new-found sophistication begins to leak out of the carriage window.

After an hour or so the countryside begins to roughen up a little and then, just south of Wakefield, I see a herd of wild clogs cavorting in the long grass – the older males sit under a tree, eating their dripping sandwiches and keeping a weather eye open for rogue whippets.

The females, of course, will have stayed at home to suckle their young and drag the old tin bath out of the outhouse and up in front of a roaring fire, ready for when their menfolk come home.

High on the night air a cloth-capped willow warbler catches insects on his way home from t'mill, and then I am woken from a deep sleep by the West Indian ticket collector, his native chant thick with the patois of his Bradford homelands.

'Wakefield Westgate – change here for Huddersfield.'

As I pushed open the front door, Arthur met me in the hall. That he should be there at all was something of a surprise. At this time of night he should have been tucked away in his cellar, filling in his pools coupon or feeding his pigeons or whatever it is he does down there.

That he should rush to greet me and bang his big bum up against my ankles was an even greater surprise. Arthur didn't do this sort of thing – he couldn't be doing with any fuss, couldn't Arthur.

And yet he raced up the stairs ahead of me as I went in search of Aileen, and then he squeezed in between us as I gave her a kiss.

'What's wrong with him?'

'He's been like this ever since you had him neutered – he's followed me around all week as though he was Sellotaped to my left leg.'

He hadn't liked being bungled off to the vet – he remembered the indignities of his previous visits and fought with me every inch of the way.

But I think he was more embarrassed about going private than anything else – his family had always been great supporters of the National Health Service and it was rumoured that his great-great grandmother on his father's side had been in at the start of the PDSA.

The vet had stood him on a rough table.

'He's a grand old chap – they make good pals, don't they?'

It was difficult to think of Arthur as a pal. I had a great deal of respect for him – he was a survivor. But it was not in his nature to show affection – he was a loner. I was allowed to feed him, but if I so much as tried to pat him on the head he soon let me know that this wasn't part of the deal.

I sat down to think it over and he jumped up on my knee. He didn't really know how to go about it and he landed clumsily, sideways on my lap.

'Ouch!'

He was a big cat and for one brief moment I thought I was now one testicle short of a set. Aileen smiled and came closer to witness this miracle.

'Maybe he's trying to tell you something.'

The next morning I was up early and sitting at my desk well before seven o'clock. After I've been away for a time I find it difficult to pick up again where I left off – but I must admit it would have been a damn sight easier with this book if it had had some sort of storyline in the first place.

I stuck at it for a couple of hours, but it wasn't working, so I switched off the computer and went for a walk and a think in Greenhead Park.

I almost had the place to myself, just me and a couple of old ladies, and it wasn't until they smiled at one another and then pointed in my direction that I realized I had company.

'Oh come on, Arthur – this is getting ridiculous.'

He must have followed me out of the house and padded

quietly along behind me, across the road and down the bank, and now he was waddling to heel across the park.

I picked him up and he wasn't too sure about that. He went as stiff as a board, so I put him down again and he followed me all the way home, right into the kitchen and up to his dish, which I filled with Whiskas Crunch.

'That was very pleasant, Deric – we must do it again some time.'

There seems to be something about me that animals find reassuring. Maybe they feel they can relax, safe in the knowledge that my company won't be too taxing for them intellectually, that they can treat me as an equal – because at the second time of trying I took a dog called Flash for a walk with me.

No, that's not strictly true – we simply walked together. I suppose with equal justification he could have gone home and told his master that he had taken me for a walk.

He was a Jack Russell terrier and he looked like a very small, brown and white Edward G. Robinson. He bounced along rather than walked and he had his name stamped on his collar.

We talked about this and that, or rather I talked about this and that and he listened. He was a very good listener and he went about it in a most professional way, with a very serious look on his little brown and white face.

As we passed by the bowling greens and approached the tennis courts we discussed Wimbledon fortnight and the strange effect it has on people.

I had never seen this end of the park so busy. All around us there were tennis players. Some of them were genuine, all-the-year-round players, and you could spot them a mile off. They had nut-brown legs and plastic covers zipped over their racquets and they carried several boxes of bright green tennis balls.

But it was the casual contestants who caught the eye. They looked more like flour graders than tennis players, and they had come rushing down to the courts because Martina Navratilova had made it look so easy on television.

Most of them wore a white shirt of sorts, together with a motley assortment of off-white shorts, a matching pair of off-white legs, black socks and almost-white plimsolls with brown laces.

They averaged three tennis balls between four of them: one green one they had picked up just outside the wire as they came in, the white one that didn't bounce too well since that dog ran off with it at Aberystwyth the year before last, and the brown one that they lost last year, but found this year when they were pruning the roses. That one didn't bounce too well either.

I watched one such foursome as I waited for Flash to complete his ablutions. He had his leg cocked up against a little sign that read *Keep Off The Grass* – apparently it didn't apply to him.

The players seemed rather taken aback to discover not only that they had to keep the score themselves, but also that there weren't half a dozen ball boys and a pair of steps, stacked with Robinson's Barley Water, waiting for them.

They formed themselves into what could roughly be described as a mixed foursome. Two women, one man and another that Flash and I weren't too sure about.

They knocked up for a minute or so, and that put paid to the green tennis ball and the brown tennis ball and left them with just the white one that the dog had run off with in Aberystwyth the year before last.

Flash had a long sniff in the undergrowth to see if he could find one for them, but when he came out of the bushes he had a baby's dummy stuck in his mouth, a big pink one with a ribbon hanging from it.

He seemed quite pleased with it but I felt a bit daft walking round the park accompanied by a small brown and white dog sucking a baby's dummy and so I put my finger in the ring and pulled it out.

'Here, you don't want that – you never know where it's been.'

'Grrrr.'

I popped it back in his mouth.

'There you are then – there's a dummy for you.'

We strolled over to the edge of the park where a line of mobile fast-food merchants plied their trade, a motley assortment of anonymous burger bars and ice-cream wagons, punctuated here and there by those proud enough to claim a little individuality.

Mandy's Fast Foods and The Chuck Wagon were professional-looking outfits, but I was drawn towards a miserable excuse for a caravan that was taking the camber of the road very seriously and leaning over the pavement to peer at its own navel.

Someone had punched a hole in the side and a large woman was handing out bacon sandwiches, but refusing to let go of them until the money was safely in her hand.

'I've been caught like that before.'

Slung underneath the hole and hanging drunkenly on a single bracket was a narrow shelf, about three inches wide.

'Don't lean on that.'

At one end, secured by a chain that had once been in charge of a rubber plug in some far off kitchen sink, was a brown teaspoon. And sitting on the other end of the shelf, secured by its own bloody residue, was a plastic tomato.

'What do you want?'

'Er – a cup of tea, please.'

'With or without?'

'With, please.'

'With what?'

'With sugar – and milk.'

'Jesus – some customers.'

She slapped a plastic cup on the little shelf and the shelf buckled. 'Are you drinking it here or taking it away?'

She had let go of the cup – it was nice to be trusted, I almost felt like one of the family.

'What's the difference?'

'Twopence.'

'How come?'

She sighed and leaned forward – the shelf flinched and so did I as she mouthed the words slowly, an inch or so away from my face so that I would understand.

'If you drink it here, you're using the facilities.'

I glanced at the teaspoon and then at the plastic tomato.

'What facilities?'

'Look,' she closed her eyes in exasperation. 'I don't make the rules – I just stand in here all day.'

Flash sat close by my foot listening to all this – what he made of it I can't think. The woman seemed to notice him for the first time.

'Do you know your dog's got a dummy in its mouth?'

'Yes.'

I should have told her it wasn't my dog, but it was too late now – or perhaps not.

'It isn't my dog.'

She didn't seem to hear me anyway. She just took my money, gave me my change and then said,

'I had a dog once that wore a beret.'

'Oh – did you?'

There isn't an awful lot you can say to a woman who has just told you that she had a dog once that wore a beret. I thought that 'Oh –, did you?' was a pretty comprehensive reply under the circumstances.

I am a very lucky man. Alan Whicker has to travel ten times around the world to meet people like this. I just walk across the road.

'Could I have a KitKat, please?'

She brought out a cardboard box from somewhere round about her knees and rummaged through the contents.

'No.'

'What have you got?'

'What do you want?'

'A Bounty?'

She checked once more and shook her head.

'No.'

'You tell me then.'

'No – you're the customer.'

After a good sort through I settled for two digestive biscuits in a cellophane packet and gave her twenty pence.

'Do I have to take them away?'

'No – you can eat those here. We have to abide by the manufacturer's recommended retail price when it comes to biscuits. It's only food what's been prepared on the premises that carries a surcharge.'

'Oh I see. Right then – I'd better be off.'

'Yes – I should be. Otherwise I'll have to charge you an extra twopence for that cup of tea.'

Flash and I walked all of two yards before we found an empty park bench. I sat on the bench and he sat facing me on the grass.

'Would you like a biscuit?'

He spat out the dummy so that he could concentrate properly and I manoeuvred it under the bench and out of sight with my foot. He ate both of the biscuits and I poured the tea away, amongst the roots of a Dutch Elm tree. It was dead already and could come to no further harm.

'Shall we carry on?'

He nodded and went under the bench for his dummy and then the three of us strolled off across the park, back towards the tennis courts.

Our mixed foursome was now spread out in a line, foraging in the flower beds like grousebeaters, and their place on court had been taken by two ladies who seemed to think that playing tennis might cure their arthritis.

One was the spitting image of Margaret Rutherford and the other could easily have been her mother. They were having a lot of trouble with their first and second serves and had worked out a system that allowed them seven serves each. Even so they hadn't actually had a rally yet.

They solved the problem ingeniously by lowering the net until it was just six inches off the ground and from that point on the game really took off as a spectacle.

Flash and I watched them for a while but then we had to be going, we were both busy men. He was anxious to show his newly-acquired dummy to his master and also to dispose of a big bowl of meaty chunks before they went off. I wanted to have another word with the lady in the caravan. There was something I had to ask her.

She was busy polishing the teaspoon and it was coming up a lovely shade of brown.

'Don't lean on that.'

I took my elbow off the shelf and stood up straight.

'You know the dog – the one who wore a beret?'

'Yes.'

'Did you teach it to do that?'

She prised the tomato away from its moorings and scrubbed at the red tide.

'No – he was wearing it when we found him, abandoned on the moors.'

My mind conjured up a wonderful image of this brave young dog, out youth hosteling on the wild moors with his stout stick and his haversack, when all of a sudden a grey mist descends and he becomes separated from the main party.

He wouldn't panic – not this dog. He soldiers on, losing his stick in a peat bog, and then, discarding his haversack as he grows weaker, he pulls his beret down about his ears and drags his aching body ever onwards until, in the distance, he hears the faint sound of a car engine . . .

'Did he wear it all the time?'

'Not the same one, no. He lost it in a fight – we bought him another.'

I fought hard against the second image – that of a small dog trying on a beret in the local Co-op.

'*I had a dog in today, Brenda. Trying on a beret.*'

'*We always have to hear about your day, don't we? You never want to hear about mine.*'

An old lady, clinging to a zimmer frame, moved in behind me and constituted a queue. The woman in the caravan stopped her polishing and picked up a large metal teapot.

'You'll have to excuse me now. Looks like the lunchtime rush is starting up.'

I eased myself to one side and the old lady took my place.

'And you say he wore this beret all the time?'

'Oh yes. Not in the house, of course – I wouldn't let him wear it in the house.'

I ran all the way home, eager to be back at my desk. What was it they used to say at the end of Dragnet? 'There are a million stories in the city – this has been one of them.' Maybe it wasn't Dragnet, maybe it was some other programme and maybe that wasn't exactly how they put it – but it was something like that.

There would have been a million stories in London. But how do you get to hear them if everybody is too busy, or too frightened, to talk to you?

I felt a warm glow of affection for the woman in the caravan and wished I hadn't poured her tea away. Live and let live, that was her motto. If the dog wanted to wear a beret then that was his business – as long as he didn't wear it in the house.

I hoped that Flash would get a similar welcome when he arrived home.

'*I like your dummy.*'

'*You're not just saying that, are you?*'

'*No, it suits you a treat – what with your colouring.*'

I could see Arthur waiting for me, half hidden on the garden wall with his big black head poking out through a hole in the hedge. As soon as he saw me coming he doubled back through the rose bushes and met me at the gate.

'*And what time do you call this? I've been worried sick.*'

He fell in step behind me and followed me up the path.

My middle name is Francis. I think it's quite appropriate, don't you?

CHAPTER ELEVEN

Aileen officially made me redundant on the fourteenth of July, at 11.32 a.m. precisely. I can be absolutely sure of the time because she pressed the little bar on her talking watch and demanded of it: 'What time is it?'

'*It's 11.32 a.m.*'

The voice is somewhat metallic and devoid of any emotion whatsoever, but when it comes to telling the time then you have to admit that it certainly knows what it's talking about. If the watch said it was 11.32 a.m. – then 11.32 a.m. it was.

For her the moment was one of triumph, another peak conquered on her everlasting climb towards total independence. For me the moment was bitter-sweet. I was delighted that she could now manage without me, but rather sad that my services were no longer required. I had enjoyed being a part of the process as she brought her stories to life on the computer screen.

With no sight whatsoever in her right eye and very little in her left, she relied heavily upon modern science, and the emergence of enhanced graphics had meant that the letters could now be blown up on the screen, until they were each four inches high, and she would peer at them and know where she was going.

Of course it also meant that there was now only room on the screen for three letters at any one time, and so it was impossible for her to read a whole chapter with any fluency.

And so several times a day the text would be reduced to normal size and Aileen would curl up on the settee with her pocket tape recorder to take notes.

Enter our hero. I would stride into her office with two cups of tea and read her work back to her, giving life to her dialogue, highlighting her gentle touches of wry humour and bringing tears to my own eyes with my sensitive interpretation of her more poignant scenes.

'You're overdoing it again.'

'Sorry.'

Then she would work at it once more, turning her words inside out and upside down, all the while incorporating the notes from her tape machine, and finally, last thing at night, I would read the whole day's work out loud to her and she would go to bed, ready to dream her characters into situations that would put the fear of God into them when they woke up next morning.

But not any more. Now modern science had gone one step further and an expert had called on us and given the computer a voice.

'Listen to this.'

She switched it on and the screen blinked blue and yellow for a few moments and then, from a little box no bigger than a mousetrap, a voice spoke to us.

'*Hello.*'

Aileen squeezed herself.

'Isn't it great? It's user-friendly you see – it's ever so polite.'

It sounded a bit of a prat to me. It could have been a second cousin, once removed, to the watch. But it was going to be a great boon to her, another giant step on the way to independence, especially on those days when I had to be away.

Even so I couldn't help feeling that twinge of regret. I had enjoyed being on the stage every night, being a part of the process that tamed and twisted the words until the book was finally brought to heel.

'I shan't have to interrupt you all the time now. You'll be able to concentrate on your own book.'

That was very true, of course. And we would still be discussing and dissecting her storyline over every meal and every cup of coffee; the computer had its limitations when it came to editorial input. But even so I would miss that light that came into Aileen's eyes when a chapter turned out to be better than she thought it was going to be.

'It's a clever little thing,' I said.

'It is, isn't it?' she agreed. 'Listen to this.'

She tapped four words on the screen and then switched on the voice box.

'*What time is it?*'

She tapped the bar on her talking watch.

'*It's 11.32 a.m.*'

Oh my God! She had them talking to each other now. It was only a matter of time before one of them learned to drive the car and then I'd be out of a job altogether.

That day and the next day I had all the time in the world to myself. No interruptions, no need to go running into Aileen's office for a break and a chit-chat, just hour upon hour of unbroken time and space to stare at a blank screen and wonder what the hell to write about next.

Through the wall, drowning out the comforting click-click of a plastic keyboard, I could hear the computer rabbiting away in a soulless monotone, and so it was a blessed relief when Jim Cochrane rang from the publishers and drowned it out.

'I've read the pages you sent me and they're fine.'

'Really?'

'Yes – rather a lot of flashbacks though, aren't there? It *is* supposed to be a year in Huddersfield.'

'I think I might be over those now. Only this past week I've met some wonderful characters – a Jack Russell terrier sucking a dummy and a woman in a caravan whose dog wore a beret.'

There was a long silence and for a moment I thought the phone had gone dead.

'You're not working too hard, are you?'

'No, I'm fine. I should be able to send you some more by the weekend.'

'You do that – I can hardly wait.'

I *did* work hard and so did Aileen. Days passed by with us simply rising, writing and retiring once again, living out of the freezer, eating stranger and stranger combinations until we hit rock bottom with the most revolting partnership of vol-au-vents and green beans.

Even so, it was late the following evening before I thought of nipping down to the shops and by that time the Mr Sainsburys of this world had long since headed for home, leaving the field wide open for the Mr Patels of this world, and probably many other worlds that haven't even been discovered yet.

(If you look very closely at that video of man's first landing on the moon, there in the distance, half hidden behind the spindly leg of the spaceship, you can just catch a glimpse of a small brown hand filling a wire rack with the early morning papers and placing a bunch of cut flowers in a bucket.)

I drove quite a distance, to a shop I had never yet found to be closed. I admired the owner tremendously – he had built up the business from less than nothing, on sheer hard work and, as far as I could gather, just four solitary words of English.

I toured the shelves and filled my wire basket, then took it over to the counter.

'Do you have any razor blades?'

'Of course.'

Those were two of his four words – there is no room for doubt in his vocabulary, however limited it might be. How he works out the meaning of, 'Do you have any razor blades?' is quite beyond me.

On this occasion, however, his optimism was unfounded. No matter how hard he shook the little dispenser on the wall, it refused to cough up a single razor blade and eventually it broke free of its moorings and came away in his hand.

He said something to me in Urdu. Perhaps it wasn't Urdu, but Urdu is such a lovely word, let's say it was.

However, since my command of Urdu falls far short of four words, we came to something of an impasse until he pointed to my beard and shook his head.

'Yes I know,' I stretched my head back and stroked the irritating grey stubble on my throat. 'It's just this bit here – I shave it every few days.'

'Ah!'

That doesn't count as one of his English words – it was a sort of Urduish 'Ah!'. The English version suggests a certain understanding, but the Urdu equivalent indicates that the utterer also intends to do something about it.

So he disappeared to do something about it.

In the meantime I mooched around the shop, browsing through the Persil Automatic, reading the small print on the back of a packet of Bold. I was just checking out my stubble in the shiny lid of a catering tin of drinking chocolate and thinking that I looked rather like a Womble, when the door opened and in walked The Hunchback of Notre Dame.

The Yorkshire version differs slightly from the original in that it doesn't have a hump – it can't be doing with such frills.

The shambling walk, however, was much the same as Mr Laughton's in the film. The back was bent and the right hand clawed, lying on its back with its fingers in the air.

The head inclined itself so far to the right that the left ear had now taken over pole position from the bald spot, and the right ear had settled down and was having forty winks on a hairy shoulder pad. The apparition shuffled over and spoke to me.

'Where is he?'

'He's in the back – looking for some razor blades.'

'Right.'

We mooched around the shop together for a while. I concentrated on cooked meats and pre-packed cheeses, while he seemed to favour the more exotic sauces and the tinned fruit.

The thought did cross my mind that he could have been genetically engineered for browsing in a book shop, but then I dismissed the thought as unworthy of me. Then it came back again, because basically it was a very funny thought.

We parted for a few moments and then, as we each ran out of shelving and swung round the end of an aisle, we came face to face once more – or at least, as near face to face as was physically possible. He looked right up my nose and spoke to me again.

'I'm not always like this, you know.'

I wanted to know more, and I was about to take the conversation on to its next logical step when the shopkeeper tapped me on the shoulder and planted a Phillips electric Ladyshave in my hand.

'Thank you,' he said, completing his tour of the English language. Then, bending down on one knee, he plugged me into a socket by the cold counter.

I am not often lost for words. Sometimes those that spring to my lips are inappropriate and often they are downright stupid, but on this occasion they very wisely decided to stay put as I stared down at the shaver lying in my palm.

This was service above and beyond the call of duty – he must have interpreted my little mime as meaning that

I needed to shave right there and then. But I couldn't have done that with a packet of razor blades, could I?

I glanced across to where he was sorting out my fellow shopper who, being Quasimodocally challenged, was having to read his shopping list at right angles.

Then I had another look at the Ladyshave. I didn't want to offend him, after all, he had gone to more trouble than they would have done in Boots, but using a strange razor is rather akin to using someone else's toothbrush – I didn't fancy it, and it wasn't even his, it was his wife's.

On closer inspection I saw that the blades were covered with a liberal sprinkling of talcum powder, and a powerful vision swept before my eyes – that of his wife sitting on the bed upstairs, waiting patiently, with one leg done and the other one in limbo.

I think I put on a pretty convincing performance over there by the cold counter. Any unsuspecting newcomer, venturing round the Paddi-Pad corner and on down the aisle in search of a little light snack for their supper, would have examined the boiled ham minutely for flying grey hairs before deciding upon its purchase.

In fact, at no time did the Ladyshave come in contact with my neck. My pantomime of a man shaving in a grocer's shop was an exquisitely controlled representation as, for once, I refused to let myself get carried away and so turn it into an all-singing, all-gargling burlesque.

I unplugged myself from the socket and went over to return the shaver, keeping my neck tucked in like a thoroughbred racehorse so that he wouldn't notice the grey hairs were still in position.

'Thank you very much – that was very good of you.'

My voice came out all dark and husky, much more macho than usual. I must keep my neck tucked in more often. The shopkeeper smiled.

'Of course – thank you.'

Quasi was having a little trouble with the door, what with the brown paper bag and a bunch of flowers under his left arm and the fact that his head was just about level with the letterbox.

'Here, let me.'

'That's very good of you.'

'To call again, plis,' the shopkeeper shouted from behind his counter and we both froze for a second or two before shuffling out into the street.

'He must be going to night classes,' muttered my friend.

Maybe he was, but only in English – there wasn't much else anyone could teach him.

I had the car right outside the shop, so I offered him a lift – though how I was going to get him in through the door, I couldn't imagine.

'No it's all right, I only live a hop, a step and a jump away.'

The step I *could* just about imagine. The hop and the jump I would have to work at.

'OK, if you're sure. Tell me something – you said you're not always like this?'

He leaned wearily against the car and rested his brown paper bag on the bonnet, the flowers nestling across his chest.

'Have you got a few minutes?'

'Yes.'

'Well – it was like this . . .'

He'd been in the pub the night before and had to obey the call of nature.

'Only the Gents' was engaged.'

'I see.'

'But the Ladies' wasn't.'

'Ah.'

Well, he hadn't seen many ladies in the pub that night, in fact he couldn't remember seeing any at all down his end of the bar.

'And it was getting urgent.'

'So you took a chance?'

'That's right.'

I've done it myself on occasions. Once, at Keele University, I was beginning to panic and there didn't seem to be any women about, so I popped into the Ladies'. And then the three hundred members of the National Women's Register took a tea-break from their Annual General Meeting and I was trapped in a stall for over an hour. I was way ahead of him.

'And you got caught?'

'No.'

'Oh.'

Apparently all was going well until he reached for the toilet roll.

'There were only two sheets of paper left and one of those was stuck to the tube.'

'It's always the same, isn't it?'

'It would have made six pieces of confetti, but that's about all.'

So he'd looked to his left and he'd looked to his right, but he couldn't see a spare roll anywhere – which isn't surprising because we all know where they keep them, don't we?

'It was stood on the cistern behind me, right in the middle.'

So he bent forward, reached out his arm behind him and felt along until his finger touched the toilet roll.

'Then my shoulder shot out of its socket, my collar bone felt as though it had snapped in half, and a muscle went in my back.'

'Ouch.'

Well, he'd sat there for half an hour or so, waiting for it to go off. But it wouldn't. One or two ladies tried the door but he didn't like to shout out, and so he hung on until after closing time and then fell off sideways on to the floor.

'I couldn't get my trousers up above my knees and my braces were caught up under my crutch.'

'So what did you do?'

'I crawled out on my hands and knees.'

'What did the Landlord say?'

'Land*lady*.'

'Oh dear.'

'She'd asked some of her girlfriends to stay behind and they were drinking at the bar.'

At first they had thought he was a drunk, but then when he explained they tried to straighten him up.

'They didn't manage it, obviously.'

'No – I've never been so embarrassed in my life.'

Eventually they called a taxi which turned out to be a mini-cab and halfway home he re-directed it to the hospital. It took them over half an hour before they managed to get him out.

'They said it was more a job for a gynaecologist – you know with . . .'

'Yes I know.'

They kept him in overnight and what with the pain and all the fuss he forgot to ring and tell his wife. She reported him as missing to the police and the first place they checked was the hospital.

'I was a laughing stock – everybody came to have a look at me.'

So he had discharged himself earlier this evening and now he was on his way home to face his wife, before she went off to work.

'It's a bit late to be going to work.'

'She's a sister at the hospital.'

He stood as near up as he could stand and swept his brown paper bag from the bonnet, then nodded sideways at the bunch of flowers in his arms.

'Do you think they'll help?'

'I think it might take more than that.'

'I think you're right.'

His brown paper bag was slipping and I steadied it for him. A dozen cans of lager wobbled slightly and a bottle of the stronger stuff poked its head out of the top.

'Drop of local anaesthetic,' he said. 'I think I'm going to need it.'

One of the flowers was longer than the others and insisted on exploring his left nostril. I eased it back amongst the bunch.

'I'll keep my fingers crossed for you,' I told him and he grinned at me through his shoulder pad.

'You do that,' he muttered. 'They're about the only bloody things I haven't got crossed.'

Aileen was still working when I arrived home. I listened at her office door for a few moments and heard Robotcop reading aloud to her. He sounded constipated.

I took the groceries down to the kitchen and prepared us a little light supper with an even lighter touch.

'I don't think much of this pizza – there's no topping.'

'You've got it upside down.'

She investigated with her fork.

'There's nothing underneath it either.'

They weren't a great success. Someone seemed to have made the pastry base and then knocked off early.

'Where did you get them from?'

'You know – that shop where I bought the chicken last week.'

That hadn't been a success either. The label said it had been spiced to an ancient Asian recipe. I had cooked it in the combination oven according to the manual, fan assisted for thirty-five minutes, and when I opened the door I thought it had escaped.

I found it eventually, skulking in the far corner, and I pulled it out and placed it on a large oval serving plate in the middle of the table. It looked ridiculous – as though all the air had been let out.

It was the sort of chicken that didn't try hard enough – it just sat there and sulked. I gave Aileen a whole breast to herself and it still didn't look enough, so I gave her the other one – and a leg as well.

'I quite liked that chicken we had last week – what happened to the rest of it?'

'I had it.'

'You little glutton.'

Over a cup of coffee and the best cigarette of the day I told her all about the shopkeeper and the Ladyshave razor. Then I pushed back my chair and acted out the saga of the hunchback of Huddersfield.

'Mr Christian – Mr Christian.'

'That wasn't The Hunchback of Notre Dame, that was . . .'

'I know – I was just getting in the mood.'

'Oh – I'm sorry.'

I hammed it up something awful, I don't know why. Aileen couldn't see my performance, but she humoured me. Perhaps that's why I do it. I like being humoured and I'm a terrible ham.

When it came to the bit about the toilet, I slumped down on the kitchen chair and reached out for the imaginary toilet roll behind me.

'Then his shoulder shot out of its socket, his collar bone felt as though it had snapped in half and a muscle went in his back.'

I stopped there – frozen in time, because my shoulder had just shot out of its socket and a muscle had gone in my back. My collar bone didn't snap in half, but two out of three isn't bad.

I lay in a hot bath for over an hour before the knots in my body began to untie themselves. Thermal sat on the end of the bath and played with the suds as usual and Aileen came in every now and then to top me up with hot water.

'Has it ever occurred to you,' she asked me as she swished the water around with her hand, 'that you might not be normal?'

Actually it had – many times. But the nice thing about being in Huddersfield was that I knew I wasn't on my own.

Later I had half an hour under the sunbed to iron out the remaining kinks and then, wrapped up cosily in my *Man at C & A* dressing gown, I switched it on again so that Thermal could have a few minutes on his own. He enjoys my company, but he likes a bit of privacy too. Aileen came up to see how I was getting on.

'So if you're fit enough, would you do me a favour?'

'What's that?'

'Will you come and read my chapter to me? This bloody machine is murdering it.'

I made us both a cup of tea and she snuggled up on the settee with her tape machine. The switch on the voice box had been turned to mute and I pulled her chair up in front of the computer and sat down, my chin tucked into my neck like a thoroughbred racehorse.

'*The Jericho Years* by Aileen Armitage – Chapter One.'

'You're overdoing it again.'

'Sorry.'

It was just like old times. A lovely woman hanging on my every word, a worthwhile job of work to do and a cat stretched out on the sunbed upstairs. What more could any man want?

CHAPTER TWELVE

As I left Stratford-Upon-Avon behind me and headed
on towards the M42 and home, I wondered what
sort of person I was.

Everyone at the dinner had been very pleasant to me,
with the possible exception of the man who had proposed
the vote of thanks to the speakers. He had been so busy
crawling up the Minister of Agriculture's backside that
he hadn't bothered to mention me at all.

Maybe I didn't deserve a mention – maybe he couldn't
think of anything good to say about me. Better the
silence than that fawning subservience that had had
everyone in the room cringing with embarrassment.

I couldn't remember a word the Minister had said; not
so much John Selwyn Gummer's fault as that of the man
on the next table.

'I don't suffer fools gladly.'

That was what he had said, and everyone around him
had nodded in agreement.

I have always thought that suffering fools gladly was
a rather decent thing to do, and by the time my mind
had stopped playing with the idea the Minister had
stopped talking and I was on next.

It seemed to go well enough, but maybe they just sat there and suffered me gladly, and if so I was grateful for that. In an exhibition room, just yards away from where I was trying to make them laugh, they had mounted a terrifying display of the sort of equipment farmers use when castrating bulls, and many of the diners were dab hands at the job.

I remembered one pair of stainless steel tongs that were so beautifully engineered and of such horrifying proportions that I made a mental note to give Arthur an extra pat on the head when I got home.

At breakfast I had been joined by a bevy of businessmen who were all agreed upon one thing.

'You must meet Gerald – he's a real comedian. He'll give you something to write about.'

They whistled him up from across the room and he sat down with us and told me thirty dirty jokes in as many minutes, all the way through my bacon and eggs and my fried bread, my toast and marmalade and several cups of coffee.

He told me a joke about a pregnant duck and then the one about the gorilla who had a limp and one arm longer than the other. His colleagues thumped the table in delight and rudely ignored the waitress who was doing her best to bring us fresh toast and coffee.

She in turn tried to ignore the one about the nymphomaniac and the garden gnome, but it wasn't easy for her and her eyes gave the game away. She turned them on me and there was far more eloquence in that one darting glance than Gerald had been able to conjure up in the past half hour.

When they left I apologized to her – something I should have done earlier, in the heat of battle.

'I'm sorry about that.'

'S'alright – part of the job.'

Maybe suffering fools gladly was just another form of cowardice – I should have told them where to go, and to take their nymphomaniacs and their garden gnomes with them.

The waitress brought me yet another pot of coffee and a virgin ashtray, still wet from the kitchen. I couldn't make out her accent.

'You're not from around here, are you?'

'No. Lincolnshire – I was born in . . .'

She told me the name of the place but I forget it. I have never quite got the hang of Lincolnshire. I have spoken in Louth twice and I was late on both occasions – I couldn't find it.

The county seems to consist of a thousand tiny hamlets, each with just half a dozen houses and twice as many chickens, and yet they all sound as though they might be towns of some substance – Honington, Leadenham, Folkingham. I tapped my cigarette in the ashtray and it spluttered and went out.

'Is that a village?'

She stopped stacking plates for a moment to paint me the most wonderful word picture of her birthplace.

'Oh no,' she said, 'it's quite large. The Co-op's got an upstairs.'

I left the table with a spring in my step and it was still there an hour later as I broke my journey and jumped out of the car to have a look at a picnic area.

After the carefully laundered conversations of the past two days, with everyone saying more or less what the other had wanted to hear, and after a diet of recycled rubbish for breakfast, the waitress had been as welcome as a breath of fresh air.

'The Co-op's got an upstairs.'

I could almost see the place. There would be a level crossing with just a single bar to stop the traffic and no gates because everyone there knows exactly what time the trains come by. A sub-post office in a converted cottage and a Co-op with an upstairs. A Lincolnshire Co-op. I'll bet you any money it had a five-speed Raleigh bicycle with derailleur gears and drop handle-bars in the window.

I had never seen a picnic area before. I'd noticed the signs by the side of the road, but in my mind I could also see a council meeting in progress where the local worthies had pondered over the problem of keeping people like me out of the real countryside – ways of shuffling me off into some sort of stockade where they could keep a close eye on me.

'We could put in a bench and some tables.'

'Have to screw 'em to the ground or they'll be off with 'em.'

'Need a concrete base for that.'

'And a litter-bin.'

'Screw that down as well – I know what they're like.'

I suppose it was a field really, a field with a tap in it. No, that's not fair. There was also a rustic table with a rustic bench attached on either side – the sort of rustic bench where the people at each end serve as bookends and you have to ask politely if you want to get out.

There was a litter-bin, a square one, and very tasteful it was too, with a council crest on one side and a picture of a squirrel on the other. The squirrel was busily eating a nut and dropping his broken shell into a litter-bin. He was the sort of squirrel a mother could be proud of.

The tap rose up out of the concrete on a swan's-neck pipe and a notice proudly proclaimed that this wasn't ordinary water – you could drink it. Another notice told me that I had been wrong about the litter-bin. It wasn't a litter-bin at all – it was a receptacle.

I sat for a while at the rustic table and looked around me. The hillside had been fenced off, leaving a sloping field that dipped down towards the main road, and in the middle, standing proudly to attention, was an ancient tree.

It was a pleasant enough tree and it seemed to be very good at its job – the council had probably sent it away on a course. Its branches were spread out wide and the roots poked up out of the ground at intervals to provide small seats for small bottoms.

There was no-one with me on my little patch of concrete, but dotted all over the field there were dozens of people, sitting on car rugs, spread out in all directions, about twenty yards apart so that they wouldn't have to talk to one another.

They had vacuum flasks and cold bags and sandwiches. Some of them had brought deck-chairs, ancient and modern, and there was a windbreak breaking wind in the far corner.

I felt a sudden desire to be a part of it all and I trotted back to the car for my camping equipment.

There was a bar of chocolate in the glove compartment. It had suffered somewhat from exposure over the months and had turned a creamy sort of white since the last time I laid eyes on it. But then some firms make white chocolate on purpose, don't they? Perhaps that's how they do it – let it mature for a couple of months in a huge glove compartment.

I had nothing to read, and my digestive juices don't work properly unless I have something to read. Then I remembered the plant I had bought for Aileen in Stratford. The lady had recommended it for its heavy scent and she had wrapped it in newspaper – pages three, five and seven of the *Sun*. It's better to be born lucky than rich. I tried to fold it so that there wasn't a bosom poking out and gave up after the third attempt.

The *Sun* has about as much idea of what constitutes a sensual woman as the *Independent* has a sense of humour, but never mind – perhaps I might find an interesting article on the European Exchange Rate Mechanism, you never know.

I made for the top corner where the car rugs were thinner on the ground. A bunch of bored sheep were peering in through the wire fence and they didn't look too happy with what they saw. They had probably paid good money for those seats and were wondering when something was going to happen.

'They don't do much, do they?'

'It's feeding time, you see – you should have been here yesterday.'

'Why – what happened?'

'There were two of them mating.'

'Where?'

'Behind that windbreak.'

I picked out a sunny little spot for myself and was just about to settle down when I noticed the rug to my left.

It was one hell of a rug, larger by far than all the rest and so thick you could have twisted your ankle just stepping off it. We've got one at home, but we call it a carpet.

It was laid out in style, as though they were expecting the boss and his wife to pop round for a sherry any minute. There was a side-table heaving with the entire production of a small Tupperware factory, a coffee table placed at an angle between two director's chairs and a well-appointed Calor Gas cooking range in the east wing.

I thought for a moment of popping round to ask if I could borrow their lawnmower, but they seemed to be rather occupied at the moment, down on their hands and knees in the long grass – probably digging the footings for the new garage.

And then in a flash, without being told, I knew exactly what they were doing. I'd done it myself on so many occasions, whenever Sally lost one of her contact lenses.

She used to lose one of her contact lenses, on average, about twice a week. We have sifted gravel from the garden path, raked out all the fluff from the vacuum cleaner and combed the lawn with our fingernails.

It was their intense concentration that gave the game away. If you are looking for a tennis ball then you can afford to adopt a more cavalier approach, but a contact lens requires all the close scrutiny of a chartered accountant going through a set of dodgy books.

What are neighbours for I thought, and so I strolled over to give them a helping hand. The woman seemed surprised when I dropped down beside her on my hands and knees.

'Neville!' she muttered.

Neville nipped round the back of her on all fours and slipped in between us, with me on his right – leaving his sword arm free to defend his wife's honour. I must show them that I meant them no harm.

'Where exactly did you lose it?'

She glared at me over Neville's bald patch. She wasn't a pretty woman and she had a tongue to match.

'We'd hardly be looking here for it, if we'd lost it over there – would we?'

That's when I should have upped and left them to it, but I suppose it was a pretty stupid question and so I gave them the benefit of the doubt. Although I don't suppose there was any doubt really – I just gave them the benefit.

We combed together in silence for a while, going over the same patch of grass several times. The sheep must have wondered what on earth we were playing at. I tried again.

'I suppose you've got it insured though, haven't you?'

Neville sat back on his haunches and considered the question.

'How do you mean – insured?'

'Well,' I said. 'My daughter was always losing hers, but she had a policy – I think it was about £12 or something like that, she . . .'

And that was as far as I got. The woman gave a cry of triumph and leapt to her feet.

'Got it.'

She ran over to the sideboard and grabbed hold of a melamine mug.

'Well, that's a blessed relief,' Neville told me. 'It was her last one, you see.'

The sheep had drifted down to the far end of the field and were trying to peep in behind the windbreak as I walked slowly back to the car.

I couldn't believe it. I just couldn't believe that I had spent the last quarter of an hour on my hands and knees in the middle of a field, combing through the long grass, looking for a Hermesetas.

As I threaded my way through the traffic and headed for Derbyshire my words kept coming back to me – like acid indigestion.

'I suppose you've got it insured though, haven't you?'

I had arranged to stop off at a village fête on the way home and I wondered what lay in wait for me this time.

I am a great believer in village fêtes. They represent the other side of life that you never hear about on the nine o'clock news.

When you think of all the people in this country who are working their butts off at any given time, for no personal reward whatsoever and certainly very little in the way of gratitude, just so that the church can have a new roof or the disabled a new bus – it makes the urban guerillas, the rabid dictators and those ranting politicians look very silly indeed.

All the same, I wondered what the day had in store for me. The most unimportant person at a village fête is the one who has been shunted in to declare it well and truly open, and today it was going to be me.

Some of the organizers can be absolutely brutal when it comes to getting their man.

'I can't, I'm afraid – I am having a kidney transplant that afternoon.'

'Oh I am sorry – what about the Saturday after?'

This time the lady had been very well organized. She had rung me eighteen months in advance and given me a choice of four alternative Saturdays, which completely blew the excuse that I would be on holiday in the Outer Hebrides.

'Who have you had to open it in the past?'

This is the sort of thing you need to know. It gives you some idea of what you are letting yourself in for – was it Princess Margaret, or was it Councillor Mrs Bradley, whose chief claim to fame was the new guttering on the hedgehog sanctuary roof?

'Let me see now. We've had Rod Hull and his Emu, and then it was Don McLean the comedian – he was very good. Then we had Tommy Docherty, but he didn't turn up, and last year we had a man who climbed up a sixty-foot pole and set fire to himself.'

That last bit of information took my breath away for a few moments and the lady jumped in to reassure me.

'We don't expect you to climb up a pole.'

She hadn't said whether I was supposed to set fire to myself or not.

Village fêtes are changing rapidly – they are being dragged, kicking and screaming, into the nineteenth century.

Police dogs display their uncanny skills as they comb a hay wagon for little bags of cannabis. A human pyramid of seventeen hefty policemen ride up and down a field on just three motorcycles and a parachutist falls from the heavens, landing on a sample square yard of bright red Axminster carpet supplied, free of charge, by Killingley Brothers (1928) from over by the new precinct.

My instructions at one fête were to declare it well and truly open the moment the parachutist hit the deck. But he was hit by a cross-wind as he jumped out of his plane and he landed up on the moors three miles away. He hitched a ride on the back of a tractor, and when he eventually arrived, an hour and a half later, the man on the gate made him pay fifty pence to get in.

But as long as the homemade-cake stall retains its prime position – just inside the main entrance and not too far from the big marquee, certainly within easy walking distance of the portable lavatories – then the village fête will never really change.

The pattern is always the same. The ladies arrive early, long before the general public are allowed in, and then they start by selling all the best cakes to one another.

Mrs Harker is in charge because she once drove an ambulance in the Second World War, so she must know what she's talking about. Mrs Cuff was only co-opted as her second-in-command much later, when we went decimal and she was the only one who could cope.

They know all about homemade cakes, do these ladies. They know that none of the locals are going to buy Mrs Pearson's treacle tarts – have you seen her lace curtains? And if she can't be bothered to scrub her front doorstep then what must her kitchen be like?

So the treacle tarts are saved for those who know no better, for the likes of you and me, along with the entire output of Miss Wolfenden's primary class, who this year have experimented with kiwi fruit and Gruyère cheese on a light pastry base.

'*She never makes them wash their hands, you know.*'

Radio Two had once given me a quarter of an hour all to myself and told me to let my imagination take a flight of fancy. I sent it off, swooping down over the village rooftops of old England – calling in on the fêtes and festivals, the galas and field days that might possibly exist if only you closed your eyes and wished hard enough. I had taken the opportunity with both hands and enjoyed every minute of it . . .

On Monday, at the National Exhibition Centre in Lower Peover, the local Green Party are organizing a Bring-and-Buy Dental Stall. If you are not happy with your teeth, bring them along and who knows? You might just find the perfect set, and it's certainly a great way to meet new people with similar interests – or at least, similar teeth.

It's Hunt-The-Midget Day at Brailsford on Tuesday and the Old Folks' Potholing Club will be performing an age-old morris dance that dates back to the seventeenth century –

it's always danced on the second Tuesday in August and celebrates the coming of the VAT inspector.

Afterwards there will be a sheep roast and wife-swapping party in the cricket pavilion – but remember, batteries are not included.

Wednesday is early-closing day in Britain, but Thursday is a very busy day indeed. This year's Frog Throttling championships will take place in Almondbury village hall, and in the afternoon, down at Brompton Regis, there is an opportunity for beginners to try their hand at the ancient art of Mole Gelding.

Now, back up to Yorkshire and the Tingley Darby and Joan Club, whose Formation Hang Gliding Team will be giving a free-fall demonstration in Wakefield town centre. They will take off at midday from the town-hall roof, go straight through the Ridings shopping centre and finish up in Pinderfields Hospital.

Later that evening, the twelfth of August, the nearby Dewsbury Irish Society will be celebrating both Christmas Eve and the storming of the Bastille.

A march past on Friday by The First Battalion of the Queen's Own Royal Chiropodists will give a vibrant start to this year's Derbyshire Miners' Rally in Wirkswirth, where Arthur Scargill will be judging samples, submitted by face workers, of embroidery, smocking and appliqué work.

There's Newt Stapling at Thorngumbald on Saturday and the local Women's Institute Nude Glee Club will be providing the vocal refrain.

Just a few miles away, in Burton Pidsea, the Cubs and Brownies will be demonstrating the noble art of tying granny knots and you can take part.

Don't worry if you haven't a granny of your own. The Cubs and Brownies are providing one spare granny apiece and there should be more than enough to go around.

Just a few tips if you haven't tied a granny knot for some time. Remember, it's left leg over right leg to start with, the spine bends forwards, and if her face turns blue then loosen her corsets and go and fetch the St John Ambulance man from the beer tent.

And before we know where we are it's Sunday and the highlight of the week. All over the country there will be demonstrations of hamster cookery by a very nice lady from your local gas showrooms.

She will show you how to stuff, pluck and kill your hamster, but not necessarily in that order.

Don't worry, there's no cruelty involved. These are specially-bred table hamsters, hand reared for this very purpose, and they love it. Just as foxes love being hunted and hares love being coursed.

She'll show you how to prepare barbecued hamster, hamster à l'orange and my favourite, baked hamsters in their jackets.

Here's a tip – try them in matinée jackets first of all. If you bake them in their duffel coats, the little toggles get stuck in your teeth.

I addressed the assembled audience from the back of a decorated float, in the company of fifty small pixies all dressed in crêpe paper, and decided that my flight of fancy hadn't been all that far off the mark.

Their little green costumes were crackling so much I could hardly make myself heard. I did have a microphone, which made a very nice change, and if only the float had had some sort of electrical supply I could have used it.

I told the organizers what a wonderful job they were doing, but I don't think they heard me – they were spread out all over the grounds, sorting out the chemical toilets and investigating complaints that old Mrs Tolbey was dealing from the bottom of the pack again.

I told the punters that they must spend lots of money, that it was all in a good cause, but the crêpe-paper kids were winning the battle and I had further competition from the wellie-chucking contest which was now reaching its climax.

I decided to cut my losses when a misguided wellie, who obviously hadn't been concentrating properly, landed right in the middle of the pixies. I quickly declared the fête well and truly open, then went off to spend a few pounds on the stalls and a penny in the chemical toilets.

They caught up with me again as I tried to guess how many chocolate Smarties there were in a four foot tall jar.

'Would you do one more thing for us, Mr Longden – would you judge the children's fancy dress?'

My heart sank. How can you possibly differentiate between little Robin Hood over there, in his hired outfit from the theatrical costumiers, and the baby Madonna with two ice-cream cones stuck on her chest and her mother's headscarf for a mini skirt?

And what about the fourteen-year-old Down's Syndrome boy who won't let go of my hand? He's ever so proud of the paper hat he's just pinched off one of the pixies.

'We've got a camera for the first prize,' the lady told me proudly, as she marched us into the big marquee.

It was heaving in there – the canvas stretched to bursting point with pint-sized knights in cardboard armour, shoulder to shoulder with embryo teenage mutant turtles. An angelic David Gower in cut-off whites and topped in golden curls battled for the sporting headlines with a two-foot-tall Gary Lineker.

Batmen and Supermen were eyeing up the Wonderwomen, while Romans in their togas kept well away from the elves and fairies who were trying to peer up their skirts. An infant strongman jacked up his muscles with a makeshift barbell, consisting of two balloons strapped on either end of a bicycle pump, while his mother yanked up his nappy from around his ankles.

'How many entries have you had?'

She consulted her clipboard, flipping over a sheaf of paper.

'Forty-three.'

'Are they split into age groups?'

'No – it's for everybody.'

'So how many prizes have you got?'
'It's a camera – I told you.'
'Yes – but what about the other places?'
'Just the camera.'

The cute and the not so cute paraded in front of me, from the baby in the pram, who seemed to have been dressed up as a baby in a pram, to the pubescent parrot, wings folded self-consciously across her tiny breasts – a seemingly endless mix of acne and nappy rash.

And beyond their anxious little faces were other faces, older faces – forty-three mothers, almost as many fathers, and a veritable panzer division of grandmothers, last seen knitting under the shade of a guillotine.

Madonna wiggled her cornets outrageously in an attempt to influence the judge – good job he was a man of iron.

So what to do? I grabbed the Down's Syndrome boy as he danced past me – he seemed to have pinched a trident from one of the Roman soldiers and he was prodding Little Miss Muffet up the backside.

I held his hand and we pondered together as the Tin Man, the Cowardly Lion and the Scarecrow passed by in front of us. I turned to the lady with the clipboard.

'Are they all from one family?'
'Yes – that's the Turnbulls.'

From her tone I gathered that she didn't think too much of the Turnbulls, but they seemed the only solution. Three winners instead of one and the camera would be there for all of them to use.

The parade had stumbled to a halt and the audience were eyeing me expectantly. The pages on the clipboard were shuffled once more and I was introduced.

'It's been a very difficult decision.'
'*We know all about that – get on with it.*'
'The standard was very high.'
'*I shall hit him in a minute.*'
'But in the end . . .'

'*Yes?*'
'. . . I decided to award the first prize to . . .'
'*Who?*'
'. . . the Yellow Brick Road family.'

If it hadn't been for Mrs Turnbull the decision would have been greeted in total silence, but fortunately for me she had been blessed with a good pair of lungs, as gipsy women often are.

'I would like to ask my fellow judge to present the first prize to the winners.'

He adjusted his pixie hat to a more dignified angle and handed his trident over to me. Then, with great solemnity, he presented the camera to the delighted brothers.

There was only one way out of the tent and I had to run a gauntlet of stony faces. I had made very few friends and well over a hundred enemies and I wished I hadn't left the trident up on the stage.

The lady with the clipboard had bravely accompanied me through the wall of silence and she stood with me now as I climbed into the car.

'What about your expenses?'

'No – I wouldn't dream of it.'

She hadn't dreamt of it either, but she had to go through the motions.

'We usually present a bouquet, but with you being a man . . .'

'That's all right – please, don't worry.'

Having got that over and done with she brightened considerably and she smiled at me as she poked her head through the open window.

'Still – I suppose it's all good publicity for you, isn't it?'

CHAPTER THIRTEEN

Aileen paused at the foot of the staircase and plucked a small white kitten out of the fruit bowl.

'I'm just going upstairs for a think.'

As she was already juggling with a glass of white wine, a pocket tape recorder, twenty Silk Cut and her cigarette lighter, I slipped the little body out from under her arm and followed on behind.

'What are you going to think about?'

'I don't know — I haven't thought yet.'

She piled the inanimate objects on the bedside table while the animate object nipped smartly under her pillow and tried to switch on the electric blanket.

'We're not getting in, Frink — we're just lying on top.'

The kitten's head popped up from under the duvet, a pink lace frill serving as a sweatband across the frowning forehead.

'*You make your arrangements and I'll make mine.*'

The kitten had a point though. It was getting much colder. I have always thought of August as being a part of summer but I am beginning to have my doubts – Nick was going to find a difference when he arrived.

My son had spent the past three years in Dubai, but now he was coming home and bringing Lisa with him. I had only ever spoken to her on the phone. Lisa Silverthorne – what a lovely name, and soon, you never know, she might become Lisa Longden. God – she must love him.

It didn't seem like three years since Nick and Jo had parted, but it must have been even longer – it was perhaps the most civilized divorce imaginable, but none the less painful for all that and I was proud of them both.

Jo had met her new man and was happy and now, after a few false starts, it seemed it might be Nick's turn. I had liked the sound of Lisa on the phone – hope she liked me.

I tried to settle down to some work but my mind was in a mooching mood, slipping into neutral every time I tried to push it into gear.

I blame the television. In my day a mind had to think for itself, but they don't know they're born these days – they can't concentrate on anything for more than two minutes together. And some of the things they come out with – it makes your hair curl. But can you tell them? Do they listen? Do they hell.

Minds aren't what they were in my day – a bit like August really.

We went back upstairs, my mind and I, looking for something to do, something that would stimulate the intellect, sharpen the senses and not take too much out of us.

I wanted to do the ironing but my mind said stuff it – it's all right for you, it said, but all I have to do is work out whether they're woollens or cottons or whatever and what sort of a job is that for a mind who once had a letter published in *Tit Bits*?

I tried to think of something more exciting.

163

'What about us taking the shower-head to pieces? We could go and get a toothpick and poke out the little lumps of grit.'

'You can if you like.'

'What are you going to do then?'

'I'm going to get in bed with Aileen.'

'You can't – she's having a think.'

'Yes – so am I.'

'What about?'

'Getting into bed with Aileen.'

We compromised and decided to save that for the sweet course. For starters we began to clear out a wardrobe, so that Nick and Lisa would have somewhere to hang their clothes.

We have four bedrooms and in each one we have enough wardrobe space to accommodate the dress uniforms and battle fatigues of the entire crew of *HMS Ark Royal*. Their going-ashore civvies, however, would have to be tucked away out of sight in a single wardrobe in the shower room – I know, because that's where I have to keep mine.

The rest of the space is taken up by Aileen's vast collection of seasonally adjusted outfits – spring in one room, summer in another and so on. Nick and Lisa were to spend the next few weeks in Aileen's winter wonderland and so that's where I began to sift and sort.

I had intended to push a few outfits forward into autumn and then shunt a few backwards into spring – but as I began to dig deep into the corners of the wardrobe I found half a dozen of my old suits shunted up to one end, like a ragged band of fugitives hiding out amongst the enemy.

They were so pleased to see me, these suits. For years they had hung there, neglected and forgotten, while all around them their flighty feminine counterparts, the cloaks and coats, the natty two-pieces, the cocktail dresses, the skirts and shirts and see-through blouses, had been taken out to wild parties and all-night orgies.

Aileen's sensible coat hung with her back to my little gang of renegades, taking it upon herself to keep them well away from some of the more frivolous partygoers, and viewing with ill-concealed disgust the plunging neckline of the Mondi jacket draped elegantly over a neighbouring hanger.

'*She's no better than she ought to be, that one.*'

And in the early hours of the morning, the split skirts and skimpy camisole-tops would hang drunkenly from the brass rail, proudly pointing out their wine stains as they recounted their adventures of the night before.

'*That's a Nuits-St-Georges, that is. He was mortified – he tried to wipe it off with his handkerchief. It took him ages – I quite enjoyed it really.*'

The thick sensible coat would have no idea what the others had been up to.

'*I don't know what they're on about – I was just dumped in the back bedroom all night with that boring wool-worsted from up Edgerton. My God she does go on, that one.*'

My little designer collection blinked at the light as I pulled them out and laid them on the bed. They must have been hidden away there for well over five years and I'm not at all sure they recognized me.

I recognized them – it was like taking a trip down memory lane, a route that burned with embarrassment as I shook them out and tried them on.

They were the remnants of my Jimmy Clitheroe days – the days when Diana, my first wife, was so very ill and I had lost so much weight from worry that the scales had slipped to a pound under eight stone.

Now I was well over eleven again and the waistbands absolutely refused to scale my hips.

'*This man is an imposter. I have never seen this bum before in my life.*'

I tugged the trouser legs up from around the knee so that at least they hung halfway decently to the floor and my shoes disappeared, suffocated in a pool of grey flannel.

Did I really wear flares like this? What on earth was I thinking about as I stood in the shop all those years ago and asked the assistant what they looked like from the back? Couldn't I see what they looked like from the front?

I tried on a jacket with a nipped-in waist. The waist nipped in, had a quick look at the job in hand and nipped out again, overcome by the enormity of the task.

The lapels seemed to have grown wider over the years, to have taken over control of the jacket in a midnight coup – they were stiff enough to repel the bullets of the most persistent sniper. Just the thing to wear with a sash and a bowler hat in some Protestant parade through the streets of Belfast.

One suit hung back as though not wanting to intrude, its dark grey cloth sober and remote. No flares, no baggy knees, no sign of shine from years of hugging chairs and driving seats.

I had only worn it once – at Diana's funeral – and I didn't try it on now. Didn't want to risk some Chaplin-esque image in the mirror – rather remember it the way it was.

I took it over to the shower room and hung it in my wardrobe, right in the middle, so that it could socialize and be a part of things, one of the lads.

But the others had to go, and I had filled a couple of old suitcases before the bed was cleared. Aileen's clothes hung still and silent, fearing that the cull might be more widespread than at first they had feared.

As I shut the door you could almost hear the deep sigh of relief coming from inside the closet.

'*Whew! I thought it was our turn next.*'

The sensible coat shook its sensible shoulder pads and tried to put the others at their ease.

'*You don't have to worry – she never throws anything out.*'

A pair of sixties hot-pants on the top shelf yawned and stretched themselves luxuriously.

'You can say that again.'

I tried to settle down to some work but then Aileen came in and told me that she had just fallen over a couple of suitcases on the landing.

'I'm sorry, I should have moved them.'

'What are you doing – leaving me?'

I told her about finding the suits and asked her if she knew where Oxfam was, at which point she settled herself down on the chesterfield and gave me the lowdown on the burgeoning second-hand clothes business.

According to Aileen there were dozens of these shops all over the place and they all seemed to be called either 'Second Gear' or 'Second Chance', 'Second Edition' or 'Second Time Around'.

'They'll pay you for them and then you can give the money to Oxfam, or Sue Ryder if you like – it often works out better that way.'

I set great store by Aileen's advice, she's got her head screwed on properly. But I had only been in the shop for a couple of minutes before I felt like screwing it off again and forgetting to tell her where I'd put it.

The window had been quite promising. A black cocktail dress, dripping with diamanté, stretched on invisible wires that you could see quite clearly. A white wedding dress, fashionably crumpled just like Princess Diana's, and a gent's natty dinner jacket complete with bell-bottom trousers, just like mine.

Several shadowy figures were inspecting the rails as I walked in, but they immediately detached themselves and fell in line behind me as I strode towards the counter.

'Let's have a look then,' barked a rather fierce voice from behind a pile of bulging dustbin liners, and then a woman appeared and glared at me.

She was wearing something that defies description, but it was in shocking pink and bulged in roughly the same places as the dustbin liners. I opened the first suitcase and tipped the contents on the counter in front of her.

The women behind me broke ranks and began to muscle in on the merchandise.

'Back,' the woman shouted, and I half expected to hear her add, 'you dogs', and then produce a whip from about her person.

She picked up my Jimmy Clitheroe number by its broad lapels, as though she was about to teach it a lesson.

'That's all right,' she muttered, and my nerves settled down and began to talk amongst themselves. 'They're coming back in, are these,' she added, and I stopped short in mid-preen.

She picked up a Harris Tweed sports jacket with leather buttons that I had bought in Sheffield one summer. I wore it first on Diana's birthday and she had said that it was like going out with her father, and since then I had only ever worn it under the cover of a heavy coat. The woman held it up to the light.

'What's that?'

'A hundred per cent wool,' I told her proudly.

'No,' she said, pointing to a spot on the lapel. 'I mean this here – is it gravy?'

The garment was snatched out of her hand by one of the crowd and the other women closed in on it like hounds around a cornered fox.

'It's blood, is that.'

'No it's not – that's red wine. You can chip blood off with your fingernails.'

'Here, let me have a look.'

I tried to grab it back and failed miserably.

'Let's not bother with that,' I suggested weakly, but they were determined to solve the mystery.

'It's Branston Pickle,' declared an incredibly short woman from somewhere around my knees. She was wearing a fur coat in August and it smelled as though it had been freshly killed that very morning.

'I never eat Branston Pickle,' I shouted and I could hear the panic rising in my voice. 'I don't even like Branston Pickle.'

We all stood silent for a few moments while she considered this new evidence.

'Well,' she suggested, 'perhaps somebody flirted it at you – without you ever knowing.'

Two questions swam to the surface of my mind. Firstly, what sort of people have friends who go around flirting Branston Pickle at one another? And secondly, did Princess Diana have this trouble when she brought the wedding dress in?

Her-in-charge had now turned another jacket inside out and was sniffing it under the arms.

'That's funny, that is,' she announced to the assembled throng, 'there's a perspiration mark under his right arm.' She had another sniff, 'But there isn't one under his left.'

She ran the test again. She was very thorough and I could feel myself breaking out in a cold sweat even as she sniffed.

'Had you ever realized that you only sweat under one arm?'

I wished I was a heroine in a fifties film so that I could I just swoon and pass out at this moment, although it would probably have been the little woman in the fur coat who caught me.

'I really don't perspire all that much,' I protested. 'I don't.'

'My husband did,' said the fur coat, staring wistfully at my right knee. 'He couldn't wear a nylon shirt, not at any price – and if he did I had to peel him out of it afterwards.'

As a group we considered this appalling scene until the woman behind the counter slammed a suitcase shut and brought us out of our reverie.

'It couldn't have been that often though, could it? He was in prison most of the time.'

Twenty minutes later I paused in the doorway with one empty suitcase and another full of rejects.

'I've just thought – you haven't paid me for them.'

It was probably the best joke they had heard in years. Dress rails rattled as people hung on for support and her-in-charge had to steady herself against the counter before she could put me right.

'You don't get that until they've been sold, love.' She came over and handed me a list. 'Try about the end of October.'

I could hear a fur coat padding along the pavement behind me and it caught up with me as I reached the car.

'You want to give them others to Help The Aged,' it advised me. 'Come on, I'll show you. It's not far.'

It was miles, and I heard the story of her life as she trotted alongside me.

'About him being in prison. He wasn't a bad man – he just hit people a lot and he didn't know his own strength.'

Help The Aged loomed up in front of us and I thanked God and prayed for a merciful release. She held the door open for me.

'I help out in here.'

That surprised me. I had a mental image of charity workers and she didn't fit the bill. I imagined a team of rather genteel ladies from the suburbs, who were doing their bit for the underprivileged and their own conscience.

'Do you?'

'Yes – I buy things.'

A rather genteel lady from the suburbs came forward and relieved me of my burden – both of them in fact. The fur coat stayed on, lurking underneath a hat stand in the corner.

I was just passing the Wimpy Bar when I remembered the suitcases and I turned back to retrieve them.

I pushed open the door and saw the fur coat on its hands and knees, rifling through a pile of suits and jackets on the floor.

It wasn't worth it – they could have the suitcases as well. I was reaching for the door handle when the fur coat spoke once more.

'It's in here somewhere,' I heard it telling the genteel lady from the suburbs, 'and it's got Branston Pickle all over it.'

Back at home I raced into the office and began pounding away at the keyboard. I didn't want to talk to anyone until I had the dialogue safe and secure, locked away in the word processor.

'. . . *you can chip blood off with your fingernails.*'

The door creaked open an inch or two and Thermal popped his head round. He smiled at me and that's when he's at his most dangerous.

'Not now, Thermal.'

He took no notice, he never does. He just strolled in, with Tigger and Arthur following on close behind. That's all I needed – a delegation.

They sat in a circle and stared at me, unblinking. It always unnerves me when there is no obvious reason for the performance. It wasn't teatime for ages yet and what other possible reason is there for living?

I told myself that they weren't really there and plunged on with my notes.

'. . . *he wasn't a bad man – he just hit people a lot.*'

The door creaked open another inch or so and Aileen popped her head in – a little higher up than Thermal had been able to manage.

'It's going to be too late if we don't hurry.'

'Too late for what?'

'To see Bart.'

'I'm sorry, I'd forgotten. Can't we go tomorrow – I really don't want to let go of this.'

'Yes, if you like.'

Aileen never puts any pressure on me, not like the cats. They sat there, three witches round a cauldron. Willing me to turn and face them so that they could lead me off to God knows where.

'Eye of newt and toe of frog. Wool of bat and tongue of dog.'

Thermal moved in a little closer and tucked himself up by the side of my foot, never once taking his eyes from my face. In a previous life he must have been a hypnotist and his powers are remarkable. Time and again my eyes were drawn away from the screen until eventually they melted in with his and the unspoken message began to filter through.

He wanted my chair, that's what it was. We had chairs, dozens of them all over the house, together with three settees that were just made for the perfect cat nap, and he wanted my chair. Well, to hell with him.

'Push off.'

Then the other two combined in a scissors movement that had me surrounded by two bright pairs of sea-green eyes and another pair in a sort of dirty yellow. My concentration, a frail creature at the best of times, decided to call it a day, and over the years I have learned that it is best to go with it.

'Aileen – I've changed my mind. Let's go.'

While his two henchmen escorted me to the office door to make sure I didn't change my mind, Thermal jumped up and took over my seat before the warmth had a chance to evaporate. He had curled himself up into a cosy ball and was busily tucking his nose under a convenient paw when Tigger glanced back over her shoulder.

'Don't forget now, Thermal – you owe us one.'

We drove over to Stocksmoor, just a few miles away, to where Bart was being held prisoner. Nick had asked us to visit, to check and see that everything was all right.

As we turned left off the main road and headed on up Thurstonland Bank Road, the countryside had a harder look about it and Aileen shuddered at the thought of spending a whole winter here.

'It's not fair, you know – six months is no joke.'

Especially when you have done nothing to deserve it. I agreed with her, but there was little we could do.

'We should have had some posters printed: "Bart Is Innocent!" We could have nailed them to the trees.'

But the trees were thin and far apart and the lanes grew narrower as we approached the main gates. I pulled the car to a halt. Even though it was still August and quite balmy in the town, a chill wind hit us as we climbed out and walked down the drive for a closer look at the Ingfield Quarantine Kennels.

We were escorted by one of the warders, a very pleasant girl who saw us through a maze of wire fencing. The dogs knew we were coming long before they saw us, but their excited barking turned to cries of disappointment as we pushed on past them and went on to where the cats were caged.

Bart looked as well as you would expect a ten-month-old kitten to look after it had been flown over from the Middle East in a small crate and then locked up with a bunch of strangers in the middle of Yorkshire.

It had cost Nick and Lisa a small fortune to send it over. However, the future here was much brighter than it would have been in Dubai without them. It was also going to cost them a pretty penny while it was in quarantine, but you try explaining that to a small chinchilla kitten and see where it gets you.

The girl opened the cage and let us in. There was quite a bit of room in there. The sleeping-quarters were high off the ground, with a grooved ramp leading down to a scratching post in the main area.

'Did you know she was a girl?'

'Yes – my son told me.'

'We thought it was going to be a boy.'

So had Nick until he had brushed her one day and found that what he had expected to be there wasn't there.

'She's got an electric blanket in her basket. She'll need it until her coat gets thicker.'

I had never seen so much hair on a cat in my life. If her coat got much thicker you wouldn't be able to tell whether there was anything in there or not. She made our bunch at home look as though they had moulted.

'We try to give them as much time as we can – but they do miss their owners.'

The staff do their level best, but they are on a loser from the start. The set-up is totally unnatural. I am all in favour of quarantine, but you don't need six months to find out whether a kitten is carrying a contagious disease or not.

The only plus about the whole business was that she was serving her sentence close at hand. When Nick had asked the airline in deepest Dubai where they thought she would be stationed, he couldn't believe his ears.

'*We always send our cats to Huddersfield.*'

We spent an hour with her. She really was the most beautiful kitten, with a serious little face and a very loving nature, and it was hard to say goodbye. She tried to sneak out of the door with us and we had to cheat on her and make a run for it.

Once outside we turned and made soothing noises through the bars, but her eyes looked a lot older than the rest of her and left us in no doubt that we had let her down badly.

The next time I came I would bring a large cake with a file stuffed in it.

I fell in love with Lisa as quickly as I had fallen in love with her kitten. They were a lot alike really. Both of them had a sweet nature and were extremely good to look at.

Unfortunately Lisa's coat wasn't half as thick as the kitten's and she shivered non-stop now that she was away from the heat of the desert sun.

'Haven't you got anything warmer to wear?'
'Yes – lots of stuff. It's all in the trunk.'
I looked around me.
'What trunk?'
'Isn't it here? We sent it on ahead.'

The shippers had no idea what had happened to the trunk. It certainly wasn't in this country, they said – could be anywhere. Maybe it had heard what had happened to the kitten and done a runner in Thailand.

We talked late into the night, until jet-lag took its toll and then they staggered off to bed. I took extra blankets in to them, but they were already fast asleep.

The wardrobe doors were flung wide open and at the far end a dozen or so hangers hung about aimlessly on the rail, unemployed and wondering where the next job was coming from.

A pure silk shirt and a cashmere jacket nudged each other as they looked out on a couple of thin tee-shirts and the two pairs of denim jeans that had been thrown carelessly across the ottoman at the foot of the bed.

'I think they must be his kids – they certainly aren't hers.'

CHAPTER FOURTEEN

I have nothing against Bernard Cribbins. I admire him and his talent tremendously. I have yet to meet Bernard Cribbins, but I am sure that if ever the opportunity arises I shall take to him instantly and have to be surgically removed from his company.

Nevertheless – I am sick of being mistaken for Bernard Cribbins. I am nothing like Bernard Cribbins. I have looked in the mirror and I have seen Clint Eastwood staring back at me.

That edgy smile, hanging around with those cold blue eyes, fidgeting nervously, knowing that it doesn't really belong and that it may be asked to leave at any moment. This is not a man to mess with: 'Dying ain't much of a living, boy.'

It's not only me – there are others who see this remarkable resemblance. That man over there who has stopped in his tracks and is bringing his tray over to my table, for instance.

I suppose it was more likely to happen in the BBC canteen than anywhere else. These people know about show business, about charisma.

'Is it all right if I join you?'

'I reckon so, boy.'

He's not at ease, but then who would be, coming face to face with Clint Eastwood for the first time?

He makes sure that his pat of butter stays well over on his side of the table, not encroaching over on to mine. He sits sideways in his chair – ever ready to take his leave should so much as an eyebrow of mine indicate the slightest sign of disapproval.

'So – what are you working on at the moment then, Bernard?'

I just can't understand it. I'm going to have to start wearing the blanket again.

It never used to matter all that much. I could always get my own back on Mr Cribbins by telling autograph hunters that I was about to star in a nude remake of *The Railway Children*.

'Jenny Agutter's playing the mother this time, as an out-of-work stripper. Just wears a G-string for most of the film.'

But now fantasy had taken a long hike into reality and a film was being made of my life – or rather, that part of it I had chosen to reveal in *Diana's Story* and *Lost For Words*.

Julie Walters was all set to play Diana and Thora Hird was to play my mother, but for almost a year now I had waited for word of who was to play me.

Clint Eastwood was out of the question of course. I couldn't see him handling the ironing scene where I do all the lace-edged pillowcases and then rush downstairs to defrost the fridge – not convincingly, anyway.

Arnold Schwarzenegger had entered into the scheme of things, but only briefly, during that period when I worked out with the chest expanders. But then he had quickly faded from the scene, the moment the nut flew off and I caught my left nipple in the spring.

Since then a dozen names had come and gone. Every time I watched television I wondered how the hero

would look in oven gloves, or whether he was man
enough to stand up to Thermal?

Now a single phone call from David Lascelles, the film's
producer, laid all the speculation to rest.

'Are you sitting down?'

'Yes.'

I wasn't. I could feel it in my water – he was going to
say Bernard Cribbins, and I reckoned that when I passed
out I should just about bang my head on the marble
fireplace and it would all be over and done with.

'We are thinking that Jimmy Nail might be just the
man to play you.'

I sat down.

That was one name I had never conjured with, not even
in my wildest dreams. He was well over six foot tall and
I wasn't. He had a Geordie accent as thick as treacle and I
didn't. He was a sex symbol and . . .

Still, I suppose one out of three isn't all that bad and
the more I thought of the idea, the more I liked it. It
would give the film a chemistry that wouldn't have
been there with a more mannered actor, and I stopped
pretending that this sort of thing happened to me every
day of my life and became very excited.

'I think it's wonderful – I think it's inspired.'

David gave a small sigh of relief.

'I'm glad you approve.'

Not that it would have made any difference if I had
objected. But a film producer has to take on problems
by the lorry-load and anything that falls off the back as
smoothly as that is to be relished.

I needed to tell somebody. Aileen had been whisked off
in a big black car and would now be in a hotel, some fifty
miles away, savaging a plastic chicken while mulling over
her talk.

'Is that the celery?'

'No – it's a flower arrangement.'

There was a sound on the stairs and Nick appeared. He

had recovered quickly enough from the jet-lag, but his T-shirt and jeans hadn't. They had a bleary look about them, as though they had just been yanked out of a deep, deep sleep.

'I've just heard who might be playing me in the film.'

'Who?'

'Jimmy Nail.'

'Spender?'

'Yes.'

He tried not to laugh – he really did. He sank his teeth into his bottom lip and held it firmly in position, but he couldn't stop the corners of his mouth from dancing up and down, and anyway the tears streaming down his cheeks really gave the game away.

'I'm sorry, Dad – it's just that . . .'

'I know.'

'I think he'd be brilliant – it's just that . . .'

'I know.'

'He's so tall.'

'I know.'

'And so – macho.'

'I know.'

He took a deep breath and tried to pull himself together. His voice was much higher than usual.

'He'd do it wonderfully. He'd capture the real feelings better than anybody I can think of.'

'He would, wouldn't he?'

'It's just that . . .'

'I know.'

He excused himself on the grounds that he wanted to tell Lisa, but I heard his lungs exploding once again as he ran upstairs and then I heard Lisa's reaction. It's amazing how she can get such a big laugh out of such a dainty body.

Over the next hour or so I rang the other kids. Sally gave a stifled yelp and told me she would ring me straight back.

It took her twenty minutes to pull herself together and

even then she talked in a strange tongue, as though she were being strangled by a close friend.

'I think he's terrific, Dad – he's got something special.'

'He has, hasn't he?'

'And with Julie Walters – it can't miss.'

'What does Steve think?'

'I don't know – he's got his face buried in a cushion at the moment.'

I rang my beautiful blonde stepdaughter, Annie. She owns *Bibliophile*, the book magazine. She has the languid looks of a cat-walk model and the raucous laugh of a Billingsgate porter.

The businesswoman and the model had gone out to have lunch together.

'Haaaaaaaaaaagh!'

What the hell do these Billingsgate porters know about movies anyway?

I rang Paul, my not quite so beautiful stepson, and at first I thought I had struck gold.

'I can see why they would want him.'

'You can?'

'Yes – the likeness.'

'Really?'

'Absolutely. You could be his older sister.'

His brother David wasn't in and Helen, the fourth of Aileen's progeny, was working out in the Middle East. I didn't ring her. She's a lovely girl but she has a laugh that makes Annie's sound like Tinkerbell. She would have thrown British Telecom's satellite out of its orbit.

What I needed was a blackboard mind, a mind that had been wiped clean of all preconceptions, a mind that would be fresh and wide open to new ideas.

'Arthur.'

'*Yes.*'

'Could you spare me a moment?'

*   *   *

He waddled into my office and propped his rear end up against the radiator. He had his usual befuddled air about him. He wouldn't have looked the same without it, but right now it was topped by a frown that hung almost down around his knees.

'I haven't done anything.'

If ever I singled him out, even just to pat him on the head, he thought that this was it – he was on his way out. He knew it had been too good to last. And winter was on its way. Oh God, what was going to happen to him now?

In a perfect world Arthur would have been invisible. Those few days when he had suddenly become the life and soul of the party were an aberration, must have been a reaction to the drugs after the vet had separated him from his manhood. Now all he wanted was to be able to sit at the back once more and pass through life unnoticed.

'It wasn't me who wee'd on the carpet.'

I told him about the film and about Jimmy Nail and how the kids couldn't reconcile his rough, tough-guy image with my more gentle nature.

'You see, Arthur, a film is a completely different animal from the book. It doesn't matter that he looks nothing like me.'

'It was that kitten.'

'What we needed, Arthur, was a leading man who could take my caring nature, my keen intellect and my sexual energy and paint it, in bright colours, up there on the big screen for a wider audience.'

'Anyway, it was only a little puddle.'

'Do you see what I mean? He's a fine writer and a fine actor, but more than that – he's become a sex symbol for millions of women, and that's just the sort of man we need if the film is to do me justice.'

'If I'd have done a puddle, it would have been a lot bigger puddle than that.'

'Anyway – thanks for listening, Arthur. It's just something I needed to get off my chest.'

*   *   *

He waddled out looking even more befuddled than when he waddled in. But that was only on the outside. Inside, I am sure he was turning over my various points one by one, assimilating and evaluating them.

It was good to see him stretching his mind. He has potential, does Arthur. We must do it more often.

Good news always screws up the writing. Bad news never does. If the police ring to say they have found my car abandoned on the outskirts of Prague and that the radio has been ripped out, the seats are all covered in blood and there's a dead body in the boot, then I can always close my office door behind me and escape into a fantasy world, filling my mind with chattering cats and kamikaze slugs.

But good news rides roughshod over everything; the excitement seeps through and dilutes the creative juices. The good news knows that I don't really want to shut it out and so it hangs around on the doorstep, peeping in through the letterbox until I admit defeat and draw back the bolts.

Of course, once it's in it takes over the whole place. Jimmy Nail was helping himself to a drink in one corner of my mind, telling the kids how honoured he was to be playing me, while I was tucked away in another corner, chatting up Julie Walters something rotten.

It was no good — I wasn't going to get a thing done. Aileen had a birthday coming up on Thursday and for all the good I was doing here I might as well pop down to town and start looking for a present.

Who knows? I might bump into somebody I know, some friend of mine who might try to drag news of the film out of me.

As soon as I turned into New Street I felt there was something different about the place and at first I couldn't think what it was. Then I saw the whitewash plastered all over one of the plate-glass windows and my heart sank. One of our shops was missing!

Another one closed down. A few weeks ago Austin Reed had shut its doors for the very last time, only for them to be opened for a day or two by a man selling suede and leather coats. He had set himself up on the pavement outside with a microphone and turned the street into a fairground with his barking. Two younger men had accosted passers-by on the pavement and tried to funnel them into the shop. After all those years of fusty service – Austin would have turned in his grave.

Now another tooth had been pulled and for the life of me I couldn't remember what sort of shop had been there before. Isn't that sad?

Until last week this empty building had been a part of the grand design. I had probably bought something from this shop but I couldn't remember what. A pencil sharpener perhaps, or maybe I had a suit cleaned.

I asked a couple of ladies and it was on the tip of their tongues. They buttonholed a friend of theirs and the four of us racked our brains together, but to no avail.

'Ask them next door – they'll remember.'

Of course they would, but that wasn't the point. I didn't remember and it mattered to me.

Long before I arrived on the scene, someone had opened these doors for the first time. Once there had been dreams of success here, three floors full of them and now, only a week after it closed, not one of us could remember whether those dreams had been built on vacuum cleaners or tea-towels.

And I would have forgotten all about old Austin if it hadn't been for the fingers of rust still tracing his name over the doorway.

It made me feel incredibly mortal. I must see more of my old friends, ring the kids every day.

'*I think I can remember him. Did he have a limp?*'

'*No – that was the other one.*'

'*I can't place him then – why do you ask?*'

'*He dropped dead last Thursday.*'

I would ring the kids again as soon as I got home.

Something stirred inside the shop and I moved in closer to have a better look. The door swung open and a man came out carrying a chrome standard lamp and a plastic bucket. A notice was being pasted on the inside of the window, right in front of my eyes. 'Everything – less than half price.'

And then a duster, apparently working all on its own, began to clear little holes in the whitewash. I peered in through one of them and saw piles of merchandise spilled all over the floor.

The fly-by-nights had moved in again and their marketing strategy seemed to have come straight out of an Oxford Street suitcase. If a policeman happened to come by the entire shop would pull up its skirts and run off down the street. I tugged open the door and went in.

The place had been gutted and just a few shelves remained, slung up haphazardly all along one wall. They were now populated by a strange and extremely colourful collection of furry animals. This lot had obviously been interbreeding for years and it showed, especially when you looked closely at the baby hedgehogs. Their mother must have been sleeping around with the koala bears. Still, they seemed happy enough and who am I to criticize? Live and let live, that's what I say.

Tastefully displayed in a child's paddling pool was a twenty-four piece patterned dinner service, in finest funfair Wedgewood, for only £9.99, and a huge pile of furry slippers slopped around in a plastic dustbin.

Fur seemed to be all the rage in here, fur and chrome. There were chrome clocks and chrome coffee tables, anoraks lined with fur fabric and a complete set of chrome chairs with fur fabric seats. I looked round for a chrome anorak but they seemed to have sold out.

I was just about to leave when I saw the disposable razors. They were neatly laid out in a series of cut-off crisp boxes and formed a fitting centrepiece for the 'Special Gifts For That Special Man In Your Life' department.

I toyed for a brief moment with a set of adjustable spanners which had been individually hand-crafted in some strange sort of soft metal. I tried one out on a chrome nut on a chrome chair and the spanner bent itself in half. I straightened it out again and quickly slipped it back into its little plastic quiver.

The razors looked all right though. I recognized the brand name and they seemed cheap enough. If I did a little bulk-buying then the kids could pinch as many as they wished.

There was a bewildering range of quantities and prices. Each crisp box contained a different offer. There were packs of six for 49 pence, five for 39 pence. You could have a dozen for 99 pence, ten for 95 pence and seven for 59 pence.

They had a pack of five for 99 pence, but they were a special twin-bladed job, and the very last box boasted a selection priced at 45 pence for three, but you got a Gerald Durrell paperback absolutely free with every two packs.

I didn't know where to start. Usually, if I know nothing about a product I buy the most expensive and hope I've done the right thing. But you can hardly call a disposable razor an investment, can you now?

Down on his hands and knees by the side of me, a young man stared at the crisp boxes. He had a baby slung across his chest in some sort of harness and he seemed to be having trouble with the prices as well. The baby was no help whatsoever, in fact I think it had just come along for the ride.

'What do you think?' he asked me.

'No idea. I've gone blank.'

We stared at them for a little while longer.

'What do you think?' he asked the baby.

'Agrooba.'

I think there was something wrong with the kid. I would have been worried if it had been one of mine. The young man got to his feet.

'Do you know, that's not a bad idea.'

'Agrooba.'

'Yes, I'm going to. Shall we ask the nice man to help us?'

I looked around for the nice man, but he must have gone.

'Right,' shouted the father, from over by a glass-topped counter. 'Shout 'em out.'

He had a calculator in his hand. It was there as a sample and had been fastened to the counter by an inch long cord, so he had to bend right over and squash the baby up against the glass to get at it. Served the kid right, I thought.

Its little woolly hat dropped off and it glared at me, backwards over the top of its bald head.

'Agrooba.'

I didn't really like the tone of the kid's voice, but I had to admit it seemed a pretty good solution.

'Six at 49 pence.'

Tap, tap, tap.

'Seven at 59 pence.'

Tap, tap, tap.

Sadly we had to reject the paperback on the grounds that we were bulk-buying and more than one copy of the same book would have been rather silly, so eventually we settled on the five at 39 pence and I bought five packs which I reckoned would last me a couple of years, or at least until our hairy brood came over at Christmas.

'Thank you,' I said to the young man. 'That was a very good idea.'

The baby nodded.

'Agrooba.'

Aileen was already home by the time I arrived and sitting by the fire in her study. I could tell from her face that the speech had gone well and she was dying to tell me about it.

One of the joys of having someone who loves you is that you can pour out all your little triumphs without resorting to the tedium of false modesty.

'How did it go?'

'I was sensational.'

Do you see what I mean? She could only say that to me. To anyone else she would have said, 'I think it went quite well.'

'So tell me about it.'

'Right. Well, I sat in the front of the car with the driver. He was ever so nice. It's his own car apparently, it's a Bentley and he does a lot of this sort of thing. Only last week he took that film star to the airport – you know, the one who's married to the tall woman who was in . . .'

I adjusted Thermal slightly and moved in closer to the fire. If we were to start with the drive up the M62 then the talk must have gone really well. Thermal adjusted me slightly and then began to pound my ribs.

Whenever Aileen has a story to tell, I love to sit and watch her face. It's a silent movie to which a soundtrack has been added. The words pick out the essential details, but the real emotion is up there on the screen. The fear when she first stood up to speak – she can't read notes, can't see the two hundred people waiting on her words – it's all there in her eyes, in the tongue that brushes up against her lips. Would she last the distance? What was it she was going to say next?

Then that first murmur of approval that turns the audience into a living thing. She can feel where they are now, almost see them. Then a laugh, from the far corner, which quickly echoes around the room and swells with warmth – no more distance, she can almost touch them now. She's going to enjoy this.

Thermal and I listened intently, eyes on the screen as the story unfolded, silent except for the pounding of paws and the cracking of ribs.

I had a story of my own to tell, about the film – but I was in no hurry. That lovely face would give the game away, sure as eggs is eggs.

Jimmy Nail – playing you?'

* * *

She skimmed quickly through the vote of thanks – too fulsome even for my ears – and then we were back with the driver and on the way home. He had smuggled himself into the bar and listened from the back of the room. He'd enjoyed it.

And that was it. Thermal and I gave her a fully-deserved round of applause and then sat back and waited for the half apologetic question that always follows these bursts of unashamed vanity.

'And what about you – what sort of a day have you had?'

I looked at Thermal and Thermal looked at me.

'*Go on, tell her.*'

I took a deep breath.

'Well – I had a phone call.'

I poured it all out. Stage managing the surprises, leaving the biggest to last.

'And guess who might be playing me?'

'Who?'

'Jimmy Nail.'

I waited, watching the face closely, waiting for it to crack up into little pieces. I didn't have to wait long and I waited in vain.

'Oh – he'll be perfect.'

She took me completely by surprise.

'You think so?'

'Yes. You remember that episode of *Spender*? He was in a room that had meant something to him once. He'd been happy there, I think – with his wife. He didn't say a word, just stood there for ages. I couldn't see him, but you could feel it all coming out of the set. The feelings, the emotions. It really churned me up. He'd be wonderful – I'm ever so pleased.'

Of course. She had only ever heard his voice. She had never seen him – not on the outside. But on the inside she could see something of me.

Thermal had run out of ribs and was now working on my left nipple. I plucked him off and placed him gently on the hearthrug.

'Do you mind?'

'Please – be my guest.'

I squeezed in beside her on the settee and put my arm around her shoulder. Now then – what would Jimmy Nail do in a situation like this?

CHAPTER FIFTEEN

I think she was surprised to see me on a night like this, what with the rain clattering down like stair rods, great chunks of it sweeping in through one end of the car-wash and straight out of the other.

The petrol pumps stood hands on hips, like ladies of the night touting for customers. They'd be lucky. Anyone with an ounce of sense would be keeping well out of it, tucked up in a warm bed and waiting for the morning.

'What on earth are you doing out in this? It must be desperate.'

'A packet of Tic-Tacs, please – the green and orange ones.'

I had left the umbrella outside, wedged upright, in between a sack of Coalite nuts and a huge bag of potting compost. I didn't want to fold it – it would have taken me and a strong lad about half an hour to put it back up again.

Helen gave me my change and a small lump from a Yorkie bar that she kept by the till. I liked it here. Silly, isn't it? There are hundreds of Shell stations all over the country, serving everything from diesel to dog food and hot coffee, twenty-four hours a day. And yet there have been times when I have almost run out of petrol just trying to make it back to this one.

It's the people, of course. I always get a smile and a warm welcome, plus a few kind words that have been roughened up a little to remove any excess sugar.

'I just fancied a walk.'

'You must be daft.'

In truth I had wanted to road-test the umbrella. Aileen had found it in Mrs Singh's secondhand emporium and presented it to me with a flourish, or with as much of a flourish as is possible when you are handling a marquee on a pole.

There are umbrellas, golfing umbrellas, enormous umbrellas and mine, and I had to be careful when I used it. In the hours of daylight I would have swept everyone else off the pavement, and in so much as a breath of a breeze I would have taken off over the rooftops like Mary Poppins.

October had been a frustrating month so far, with no rain to speak of and high winds that had turned Arthur's fur-coat inside out and blown Tigger right off the rockery.

And so tonight had been sent from heaven, in more ways than one. You see, when I have something new I just can't wait. I need to try it out there and then, tomorrow is far too far away. Aileen and I had once staged an impromptu sing-song around the new piano while it still sat in the back of the removal van.

As I walked back home the rain bounced high off the pavement and ran like a river in the gutters, bubbling up round the tyres of parked cars. The grass over in the park had begun to sweat profusely, the surface water glistening in the moonlight now that there was only room on top.

I felt like a little lad in a new pair of wellies, looking for puddles to stamp in. Only there weren't any puddles around me – I was a mobile dry spell.

As I neared home an overhanging branch forced me out towards the pavement edge and my umbrella completely covered a small Citroën that had been hitched up to the kerb for the night. It stirred slightly and for a moment I thought it was going to wake up, but then it just had a little stretch and dropped off back to sleep again.

There was a woman ahead of me. She had something on a lead and unless hamsters have started barking I had to assume it was a small dog. It wasn't a particularly happy little dog. The rain was bouncing up off the pavement and attacking it from underneath.

It didn't take me long to catch up with them and I wondered why she should be out in this weather at one o'clock in the morning, in a skirt and thin jacket and with no umbrella.

I moved in on their heels to offer assistance but the outer perimeter of my umbrella arrived there slightly ahead of me, shielding them from the rain, and I was just about to say something when they stopped dead in their tracks.

The woman stuck out her hand to see why it had stopped raining and the dog sat down on the wet pavement and looked puzzled. He could still hear it but he couldn't feel it any more.

'There's plenty of room under here for all three of us.'

At the sound of my voice the woman swung around and stared at me for a second or so. The dog, being on a short lead, did exactly the same – only he had no choice in the matter.

She was much older than I had thought she would be, or perhaps she had just aged ten years in that very moment. She must have been at least seventy. I smiled my comforting, good Samaritan's smile at her and she threw her head back and screamed a scream that came straight out of a Hammer Horror movie.

I don't frighten people on a regular basis, in fact I can't even remember having frightened anyone ever before. It's not a nice feeling. I put a reassuring hand out towards her shoulder and the movement galvanized her into action.

She turned and started to run at one and the same time, sheer terror turning her into a facsimile of Linford Christie.

The little dog hadn't even turned round yet but the lead saw to it that he had to go as well, and he had already covered the first three yards or so on his back before he managed to right himself.

Unfortunately the lead had wrapped itself round his two front legs and tied them together, so that the woman dragged him along with her as she ran. I watched him disappearing into the distance, tobogganing along behind her on his stomach, bumping up and down on the uneven stone pavers.

I had to do something. If I chased after her she might have a heart-attack, so I nipped across into the park and passed them on the other side of the road, under cover of the bushes.

The umbrella — got to get rid of the umbrella. I dropped it down by the side of a tree and it spun like a top, then I strolled casually back across the road, whistling a merry little tune and trying to look awfully respectable as the two of them panted along on the other pavement. As soon as she saw me she shouted, 'Oh thank goodness.'

'What is it?'

'There's a man . . .'

She couldn't say any more. She leaned against me, pointing up the road and trying to get her breath back. The dog rolled over on to his back and tried to examine his scorch marks as he untied his front legs.

'What about this man?'

Well, apparently he was much taller than I was and a lot younger. You could tell he was the violent type and she'd recognize him if ever she saw him again. He had this huge umbrella with him.

I had been about to confess all, but now it seemed that the right moment had passed.

'Look, that's my house over there – would you like to have a sit down until you recover?'

She wouldn't, but she would appreciate it if I walked her home. I offered to get the car out but she said the dog didn't like cars. He didn't seem to like me either – I think he was beginning to put two and two together, now that he'd got his legs sorted out.

She lived well over a mile away and she wasn't the fastest of walkers. The dog was even slower than she was and I ended up carrying him on the last leg of the journey.

On the way home I stopped off at the park to pick up my umbrella, but it was nowhere to be seen. I remembered dropping it by the foot of a tree, but one tree looks very much like another in the dark and in the pouring rain.

I would have another look in the morning. I just wanted to get home now. As I walked up the garden path, the security lights came on and I took a good look at myself.

I was soaked to the skin and my shoes and trousers were caked in mud from the park. I tried to clean myself up as best as I could in the porch, but the security lights are on a time-switch and so, in order to see what I was doing, I had to keep running up and down the path every couple of minutes until they came back on again.

It was almost half-past two by the time I went upstairs. Aileen was sitting up in bed, half asleep, waiting for me. I bent over and gave her a quick cuddle.

'You've been ages.'

'I know – I'm sorry.'

'You're wet through.'

'It's nothing really.'

'Why didn't you take your new umbrella with you?'

If she hadn't dropped off to sleep I would have told her the whole story. As it was I sat quite still for about ten minutes before I removed her head from my shoulder and then laid it down gently on to the pillow. My right arm was fast asleep now and it was about time the rest of my body joined it. Aren't heads heavy when they have dropped off?

I peeled myself out of my wet clothes and crawled in beside her. She stirred slightly as a damp foot caught her on the bare bottom and she muttered something in a half-baked monotone.

'I can't hear you?'

'Did you remember my Tic-Tacs?'

'Yes – but I gave them to a small dog who looked like a hamster.'

She didn't hear me – she was fast asleep again. Sometimes I get off very lightly.

The next morning I cut through the park on my way into town and searched around for the umbrella. For a moment I thought I could see it through the trees, but it was a false alarm – it turned out to be the roof of the bandstand – so I gave it up as a bad job and began practising my excuses for Aileen's benefit.

The bowling green was flooded. It's set in a little dip below the tennis courts and a small duck bobbed along on the waves, quacking obscenities at a bunch of sparrows who were having a stand-up wash in the shallow end. You would have thought the duck had lived here all his life. He had taken to it like a duck to water.

The sparrows told him to push off and the duck wanted to know who said so and the sparrows told him that they said so, and so he paddled up to my end where a woman immediately began chucking him large lumps of bread from out of a Mother's Pride wrapper.

'I'm thinking of getting up a petition,' she told me. 'Would you sign it if I did?'

'What sort of petition?'

She nodded towards the duck, who was now standing on his head and waving his bottom at us.

'They're going to pump it dry if it hasn't all gone by tomorrow,' she said. 'It's not right, is it? Destroying his natural habitat.'

Destroying his natural habitat? He couldn't have been there for more than a couple of hours. I did mention this to the woman, but she wasn't interested in small details like that, so I left her to it and headed off towards the library.

I wanted to check out a story about a brass band, and the staff are very helpful down there. What they don't know about local history isn't worth knowing.

Huddersfield has a fascinating past. It was owned lock, stock and barrel by the Ramsden family right up until 1920, when the town council bought it, rather surreptitiously, through an Australian go-between. It was the last town in England to buy itself from a feudal landlord and if you want to know more about it you ought to try reading *Hawkrise*, by Aileen Armitage. It's very good and I should know – I sleep with the author.

The library staff have helped us greatly in the past with stories about the Luddites and the Chartists. Brass bands would be a doddle. Ask them where Marks & Spencer's is and they haven't got a clue.

I had heard the story in a pub one night, told by the man who knows everything. There's one in every pub. He might never have been further than the end of their yard but he possesses an unnerving self-assurance that would make even a passing astronaut feel that he had led a somewhat sheltered life.

'You don't know where Brook's Motors is?'

'No. But I have been to the moon.'

That wouldn't carry any weight with the man who knows everything. He'd take a long pull at his pint and slowly wipe the froth from his top lip.

'Well – you could hardly miss that, could you?'

I had lent half an ear to him all evening as he sorted out pestilence and famine in the Third World, equating its problems to those facing Barnsley just before the First World War. But then I swung my chair around and joined in when the conversation turned to brass bands. Here was something he might know something about.

He waited impatiently while a younger member of the group told of the night he sat in with the Brighouse and Rastrick. The young man's eyes shone as he recalled the fear and excitement of the occasion, as he told of how the masters of the art had nursed him along until he had achieved more than he ever thought possible.

The man who knows everything waited for an appreciative pause from the others and then punctuated it with a long drawn out sniff, a drayhorse of a sniff that told the others the spotlight had been off him long enough and could he have it back, please. He took another long pull at his pint and leaned forwards in his chair.

'There were this brass band once. Won everything they went in for, they did, in the early nineteen-hundreds.'

'From round here, were they?'

'No – from over towards Penistone. Won everything in sight for years on end and then they just seemed to disappear off the face of the earth.'

'Why was that?'

'That's what I wanted to know.'

'And?'

He poured himself another pint from a jug on the table.

'I had a word with someone who'd been on the committee and apparently it were tradition that killed 'em off. Every time a bandsman died they buried him with his instrument and eventually they had now't left to play.'

It was a story I had cherished from that day on. But the very thought of a man being buried with his french horn laid out beside him stretched the imagination as much as it would have stretched the churchyard's resources.

The library staff said they would give me a ring if they found anything and so, after a quick check through the shelves for the simple pleasure of seeing myself snuggling up, shoulder to shoulder, with Lord Longford, I nipped across to Choosy's for a well-earned cup of coffee.

I browsed around in the shop downstairs for a while, inhaling the wonderful aroma until I could take it no longer. I charged upstairs, ready to kill for a cup. They're not daft in there.

I picked an empty table in the smokers' corner, ordered myself a cafétière of their finest Colombian coffee and then lit the first cigarette of the afternoon. It was three minutes past twelve and I was ready for it.

It wasn't until I lowered the newspaper to pour my second cup that I realized he was there. It was as though he had been greased into place. I certainly hadn't heard him arrive, but then I never did. Every time I set foot in the café he simply appeared in the chair opposite as if by magic.

The first time had been a few weeks ago and I had tried my hand at a little pleasant conversation. I discovered that he worked as a counter assistant in a wholesale warehouse and that they had a canteen over there, but he liked a saucer with his coffee so he came over here.

And that, as far as conversation goes, had been that. Since then he had sat opposite and stared at me in silence, through bottle-bottom glasses that had to be de-steamed every few minutes on the sleeve of his anorak.

His problem was that he sat too far forward in his seat, with his neck turtled over the rising heat from his coffee cup. His lenses would first steam up at the outer edges, and I would sit, fascinated, waiting for the effect to spread.

It was quite exciting to watch as they clouded over, the steam moving slowly inwards, carefully feeling its way along until it got the hang of it, and then joyfully stepping up the pace as it raced to meet up in the middle.

I would have thought it would have started in the middle and then moved outwards – life's full of little surprises, isn't it?

*   *   *

He looked as though he had been born in an anorak. I could imagine him sitting up in his pram, resplendent in his little matinée anorak and then I would see him a few months later, switching to one of the more fashionable Baby-Gro anoraks as he learned to crawl.

Thoughts like this are the first sign of madness, so I poured the coffee, added three sugars to taste, and settled back behind my newspaper and tried to concentrate.

It wasn't easy. I could feel his eyes boring through the newsprint and then, to my great surprise, for the first time in a long time he spoke to me, haltingly, as though I might slap him across the face for his effrontery.

'I'm going to Ipswich tomorrow.'

I lowered the newspaper to see if he was really talking to me and he was, but the effort had taken it out of him and his glasses were steaming up again. He whipped them off and wiped them on his sleeve. I felt I ought to say something.

'What's going off in Ipswich then?'

The spectacles were slotted back behind his ears and the thick glass seemed to magnify the panic in his eyes. He grabbed his holdall from in between his legs and stood up.

'I must be going – I've said too much already.'

And with that he was off, halfway down the stairs, leaving me with my mouth wide open and a whole host of questions left unanswered.

I turned these questions over in my head as I traipsed up Trinity Street on the way home. What the hell was he going to do? Plant a bomb? Start a fire? Should I inform the police?

Perhaps he *was* the police – perhaps he was in Intelligence? No, that was ridiculous. I would keep a close eye on the papers and the television news. If anything happened in Ipswich I could be on *Crimewatch* next week.

*   *   *

It began to rain once more as I reached the park gates. At first it was only slarting it down as they say around here, that is, when all you can see of it are those little broken lines on the window-pane. But very soon it was siling it down, as they also say around here, and that is when it falls in big lumps on your head and you wish you hadn't lost your umbrella.

Perhaps I hadn't. It was coming across the park towards me, tottering along on a pair of bandy legs and weaving a drunken path as the occasional gust of wind played games with it.

I was going to have to tackle whoever was underneath. I had another look at the legs and they looked a lot shorter than mine. They looked a lot older as well. That was all right then. I could afford to be firm – if he was really old I could beat him up.

'Excuse me.'

No reason why I shouldn't be polite, but at the same time there was a firmness about my voice that would leave him in no doubt as to who was in control of the situation.

'Where did you get that umbrella?'

The front end tipped up and I stepped underneath and joined him. If I was going to beat him up I might as well do it in the comfort of my own umbrella.

He smiled at me. He didn't seem to realize that I was being firm. Cocky little devil. He looked about seventy and my confidence was growing all the time.

'Mrs Singh's,' he said. 'It's a second-hand shop up Marsh – she's got dozens of them. They're only three pounds fifty each.'

I stared at him, eyeball to eyeball, one either side of the wooden handle. I'd moved in close because I thought it might be more intimidating.

'Thank you very much.'

'My pleasure.'

He raised the umbrella as high as his little arms would allow and politely let me out of the back door. I smiled grimly to myself as I strode across the sodden turf – he had no idea what a narrow escape he'd just had.

I pushed open the front door and slotted my new umbrella in behind the coat-rack. Mrs Singh had been sworn to secrecy and Aileen would never know. Three pounds fifty. My wife really knows how to spoil a chap.

She came down the stairs from the office with a small white kitten under her left arm. You could tell from the body language that this kitten had been a very naughty kitten indeed. The woman's chin was set in a firm line that extended right down her neck and across her shoulders.

'I've just about had enough of her.'

The kitten's body language was on a much smaller scale, the kitten's body being much smaller, but nevertheless it spoke volumes.

'*I think she's just about had enough of me.*'

Behind them, on the stairs, sat three other cats. It isn't possible for cats to sit with their paws on their hips, stewing with indignation, but if it could have been done, they would have done it.

'*We've just about had enough of her.*'

Aileen held Frink out to me at arm's length and I took delivery of the little body.

'Do me a favour – stick her in the cellar for a while.'

That isn't anywhere near as cruel as it sounds. Half the cellar has been done out as a basement flat and Frink would have the run of it until the rest of the household decided to forgive her.

That could be anywhere between a couple of minutes and a couple of hours and in the meantime she would have a shower room all to herself. She could pick out a tune on the piano if she wished, browse through the bookshelves or have forty winks in an easy chair. We also have a wine cellar down there, so I made sure that the corkscrew was well out of her reach.

She isn't a bad kitten. She just has more energy than all the rest of us put together and a spell in the sin bin would do her no harm whatsoever. It would do the rest of us a world of good.

I switched on the light at the top of the cellar steps. It's one of those early fluorescent strip lights and it likes to take its time. It was still trying to remember what it was it was supposed to be doing as Frink and I blindly negotiated the first landing and picked our way down the second flight of steps.

It had just cleared its throat and begun humming in a more confident sort of manner when I reached the bottom step and planted my foot into a good three inches of water.

It wasn't what I was expecting at all and I pitched forward, catapulting Frink through the air. I heard her land with an almighty splash and then the light came on and I saw her, doing a passable breaststroke towards the piano on the far bank.

The cellar was in one hell of a mess. All five rooms were completely flooded and a tidal wave zipped across the floor of my workroom, driven by a draught through the flapping cat-flap and the water that poured down the cellar steps.

Frink was in her element. She's a Turkish Van cat and her ancestors were swimming cats from Lake Van. We have the devil's own job keeping her out of the sink when we are washing up and it's only because the Fenjal makes her eyes water that she doesn't join me in the bath.

I left her to it and went off in search of my wellingtons. She did a bellyflop from off the top of my Black & Decker Workmate and went in search of a ping pong ball that she keeps down there for when she is in solitary confinement.

She might not be on her own for long. News travels fast in this part of the world and word had probably reached the bowling green by now. I wouldn't be at all surprised to find that the duck had joined her by the time I got back with my mop and bucket.

It took two full days to clear up the mess and another two weeks before we were able to start putting things back. The land drains in the garden had been unable to cope and we had them de-silted by a man who knows about these things.

'You're lucky it wasn't the sewers.'

It was nice to be lucky, but I hoped I wouldn't be this lucky too often.

By way of celebration I nipped down to town to do some shopping and on the way home I called in at Choosy's for a coffee.

I wanted to see if Anorak Man had returned from Ipswich. I had to know what he had been up to and my heart leapt when I saw him sitting at a table in the corner.

As he wiped his spectacles on his sleeve I slipped into the chair opposite, and by the time he had the bottle-bottoms back on the end of his nose I was already grinning in at him through the other side of the thick glass.

'How was Ipswich?'

He looked nervously around him, checking for prying eyes and eavesdroppers. In his business you couldn't be too careful. He leaned forward and whispered to me in a thin, reedy voice.

'Promise you won't tell?'

I shook my head.

'No – I won't tell.'

His left eye twitched nervously. It seemed about a foot across.

'Well – I borrowed this loudhailer from work.'

'Yes.'

'And then I drove down to Ipswich.'

'Right.'

'And went all round the back streets.'

He hesitated. Was he wise to let me in on his secret?

'Then what do you do?'

'Then I wind down the windows.'

'Yes.'

'And what I do is, I shout . . .'

He cupped his hands around his mouth to simulate the loudhailer.

'. . . your water will be cut off at 3 o'clock for eight hours.'

I sat and stared at him – I couldn't believe my ears. And then I began to laugh at the ridiculousness of it all and he took this as a sign of encouragement. He sprang to life for the very first time and began to count out the towns on his fingers.

'I've done Blackburn, Barnsley, Burnley . . .'

As I walked home I thought it over. This was his hobby – this was what he did for kicks. And yet he couldn't see the panicking householders as they topped up their kettles, filled their baths and buckets in readiness for the drought to come. He'd be long gone. What did he get out of it?

Soft lights glowed in the windows of the terraced houses as I passed by. What really went on behind those lace curtains, I wondered? What did they get up to when no-one was looking?

And then the first drops of rail began to fall, and around me a whole army of matchstick men and women set about raising huge umbrellas, dozens of them, just like mine. Mrs Singh must be making a fortune.

CHAPTER SIXTEEN

Thermal sat on the chair across the table from me and frowned his special frown. This wasn't how first thing in the morning was supposed to be. First thing in the morning was supposed to be just me and him. Or as he would have it, him and me.

But this wasn't first thing in the morning. This was second thing in the morning and I had overslept and the rest of the household had caught up with us. Tigger sat on the chair between us and Arthur stood on all fours over by the sink and head-butted the kitchen door.

Arthur woke every morning convinced that he had been trapped overnight in the house against his wishes. He had to get out – he was a free-range cat, a free spirit, and so he banged his head against the door where there would have been a cat-flap if we had had a cat-flap in that door, and tried to get out.

I let him out and then waited with the door wide open. He raced once around the courtyard in the pouring rain, his bladder bursting, while I picked up the milk bottles.

'I'm closing the door, Arthur.'

He came racing back in and shot upstairs to use the

cat litter tray. Sometimes I think I may have pushed him too hard with my lessons on feline etiquette.

Back at the table Tigger sat and worshipped me. Every now and then she goes through a phase where she thinks I am the most wonderful person on earth and I find it acutely embarrassing.

'Just look at the way he holds that slice of toast, Thermal – just look at those long delicate fingers.'

Thermal took no notice. He had spotted a rogue cornflake hiding by the side of the marmalade jar and was lulling it into a false sense of security by completely ignoring it.

'Look at the way he extends his little finger when he picks the crumbs off his chest. It shows breeding, does that.'

She never took her eyes off me, just fluttered them every now and then, opening and closing them in sheer adoration. As I picked up my copy of *Publishing News* I fluttered back at her and she almost fell out of her chair in a spasm of ecstasy.

I could hear Bridie, out in the hall, singing an old Irish folk song, accompanying herself on Panasonic vacuum cleaner and feather duster.

Not content with cleaning her own Albert Hall of a house just across the back lane, she had long ago decided that there was no way we could manage without her services and had now taken us over lock, stock and barrel.

She broke off in mid-ballad and burst into the kitchen, followed immediately by the mild-mannered Chico Mendes O'Connell who works as her personal ginger tomcat and resident straight man.

'Don't stop singing, Bridie. I was enjoying that.'

She emptied the cleaner bag into the pedalbin.

'I've forgotten how it goes now – the song just split open and the words fell out.'

I treasure Bridie's way with words. Just before Yugoslavia

went and split itself wide open she flew over there to visit a statue that is reputed to weep real tears. Aileen hates flying and wondered how Bridie had coped with the flight. She had found it no problem whatsoever.

'I just stayed up there until the plane came down.'

She patted Thermal affectionately on the head and his neck folded in on itself like a concertina. She has a heavy hand and I am sure it accounts for many of Chico's psychiatric problems – his nervous twitch at least.

I still can't help feeling terribly guilty about having someone else tidy up around me and I apologize like mad. Half rising to my feet, I explained.

'I overslept – I was going to make an early start.'

She patted me on the head as she swept back towards the hall.

'Don't you worry about it. There's nothing taken out of tomorrow yet.'

I felt much better for that piece of information and so, after massaging my neck back into its original position, I poured myself another cup of coffee and opened my *Publishing News*. A few more minutes wouldn't make any difference, there was nothing taken out of this afternoon either.

As I settled down to read a review of the forthcoming hardback books, Thermal rose nonchalantly to his feet and gave a big, big, stretch. The cornflake took no notice. Poor little sod – it was probably a very young cornflake, still wet behind the ears, and had no idea that this was merely part two of a well-rehearsed manoeuvre that Thermal has perfected over the years.

He was growing up, was Thermal. It would be his third birthday next week. I must buy him a present. Something different – something he wouldn't normally buy for himself.

I was just trying to think of something he would really like when everything seemed to happen at once.

Just as Thermal launched himself at the cornflake, I spotted the title of Alan Coren's latest book.

'Damn it!'

Thermal seemed to think I was shouting at him and tried desperately to abort his deadly mission in mid-air. He banked sharply to the left, but the angle was too tight for him and he couldn't get the lift. He crash-landed on top of the jar of marmalade and Tigger panicked and jumped from her chair, landing right on top of Arthur who had come downstairs to sort Chico out for eating his breakfast.

The jar of marmalade was furious. It steam-rollered its way across the kitchen table, barging through a picket line of teaspoons until it came across the sugar bowl. It had never liked the sugar bowl and now seemed as good a time as any to settle old scores.

The sugar bowl just wasn't concentrating. It had no need to – breakfast was a meal it had done a thousand times before, it could do breakfast standing on its head – and in no time at all it *was* standing on its head and then on its feet again as it hurtled through the air, spinning ever downwards in ever decreasing circles until it broke into a dozen pieces on the unsuspecting Arthur's head.

I don't think it hurt him too much but it certainly wasn't his day. He shot out of the kitchen, covered in sugar from top to tail, looking for all the world like a cat with terminal dandruff, right between Aileen's bare legs as she entered the kitchen stage left.

'What's going on?'

I told her what had happened as she crunched across the kitchen floor and continued with the explanation as she degranulated in between her toes with a screwed-up plug of kitchen roll.

Bridie had heard the crash and came running at a slow trot, hoping that whatever it was that had happened would all be over by the time she arrived.

'You're never cleaning that lot up with a wet cloth?'

'I was just . . .'

'Ah leave it to me, you'll have us stuck to this floor for a fortnight.'

I made Aileen a cup of tea as Bridie went to work with a dustpan and brush and then I sat down at the other side of the table and picked up the *Publishing News* once more. Bridie flicked away on her hands and knees, her head nudging up to the leg of my chair.

I pulled my dressing gown tight around me, crossed my legs for extra protection, and then began to read the bad news.

'Alan Coren has a book coming out . . .'

'Now don't you mind me.'

'. . . published by Robson Books . . .'

'Just you pretend I'm not here.'

'. . . and do you know what he's gone and called it?'

'I'll be as quiet as a church mouse.'

'He's called it *A Year In Cricklewood*.'

Aileen made all the right noises, sympathy oozing from every pore as her tentative hand combed first her place mat and then the surrounding area, searching for the slice of toast that I was going to make her as soon as I had finished my cup of tea.

'Oh that's rotten.'

Bridie wasn't so sure. She considered the matter as she squatted on all fours beside me.

'I quite like it myself. It has a ring to it. I wonder what it's about? Could be about a year in Cricklewood, I suppose.'

I turned the problem over in my mind as I followed Arthur round the house with Thermal's brush and comb set. The title of the book had been the only thing I had settled on so far. 'A Year In Huddersfield'. It wasn't much, but apart from the odd chapter and a pile of notes it was all I had, and now Alan Coren had gone and beaten me to it and I was going to have to have a re-think. It was one thing to write a parody of Peter Mayle's *A Year In Provence*, but quite another thing to write a parody of a parody.

Out in the hall I spread a double page from the

Independent on the floor and Arthur came over and sat on it. He never could resist the sensual feel of warm newsprint up against his bare bottom. He screwed his head right round until he had it on back to front and then he began to lick the sugar from his left shoulder. His face was a picture of sheer disgust. He hadn't got a sweet tooth, hadn't Arthur – or if he had it had fallen out years ago along with all the others.

He put up with me and my comb until the moment I touched that nerve on his spine which has become so highly sensitive since he had both his back legs broken, and then off he trotted to find a more private venue in which to tackle his important little places.

What the hell could I call the book now? It had to have a Yorkshire feel about it. 'The Silence Of The Whippets' perhaps, or 'Death On The Carlisle and Settle Express'. I thought about what I written so far and *Much Ado About Nothing* immediately sprang to mind.

I followed Arthur up the stairs and found him sitting under the telephone table on the office landing. He had one leg stuck high in the air, very much as Nureyev might have done had he spent his early days living out of the dustbins in Brighouse.

He worked his tongue from stocky thigh to pointed toe in the approved manner and his black fur glistened even more than usual as the sugar and the saliva teamed up to form a hardy crust that would probably preserve his leg for posterity.

'No – I'm afraid Arthur died years ago, but we still have one of his legs in that tall jar over there.'

He paused for a moment, admiring the shimmering limb that still pointed towards the heavens. He seemed reluctant to bring it back down to earth, or perhaps he couldn't shift it without it cracking.

I laid another double sheet of newspaper on the floor, this time on the Chinese rug, and the twin lure of cosy newsprint and exotic underlay proved too much for him. He chose the racing page and limped over to park his bum on Willy Carson while I combed the sugar out of his Rastacat tresses.

Thermal hove into view up the stairs and then came over to have a closer look at what was going on, settling himself down gingerly on the television listings.

I felt like a barber, with one in the chair and one waiting. I leaned over and whispered in Arthur's ear.

'Anything for the weekend, sir?'

Jokes are wasted on cats but I enjoyed it, much more than Arthur was enjoying the grooming. The sugar was beginning to coagulate now and the fine-tooth comb was getting bogged down in a thick syrup. By morning I was going to be the proud owner of a crystalized cat.

He'd just about had enough. With great dignity, or with as much dignity as a cat can muster when it's just been freshly glazed, he waddled off down to the kitchen to find himself a quiet place where he could finish his ablutions in peace and maybe nibble a little Whiskas on the side.

'Next, please.'

Thermal usually rather enjoys a quick shampoo and a set but one look at the sticky comb was enough for him. He turned on his heels and hobbled off towards Aileen's office and its comfy settee. I watched him limp away and wondered if it was catching, then turned back and saw the bloody paw-prints on the newspaper.

'Thermal?'

For a cat with a raw paw he certainly took some catching, and there ensued a good five minutes of huffing and puffing before I had him cornered in the shower tray on the third floor.

'Let's have a look at you.'

It's not always easy to tell with a cat where a wound starts and where it finishes. The fur complicates matters and things can look worse than they are, but in Thermal's case the diagnosis was simple. His paw was split wide open and it was going to need some stitches. I picked him up and gave him a cuddle and he butted me under the chin with his head.

It's at moments like these, when no-one is looking, that two chaps can simply be themselves – can cast aside the restrictions that a narrow-minded society thrusts upon them.

And so, while the one with two legs murmured sweet nothings and stroked his fingers down the soft and velvety back, the furry one soaked up the sympathy and dribbled blood down the front of my shirt.

The shower tray already looked as though someone had recently slaughtered a chicken in there, and as I carried him down three flights of stairs I could see that the carpet had been rubber-stamped with a trail of single paw-prints all the way up. And now my shirt was being dyed a rich ruby red all the way down the front.

It was the sugar bowl of course. He must have landed on a sharp bit as he tumbled off the table. Bridie had found further evidence on the kitchen floor and was examining Aileen's bare foot to see where the blood had come from. Aileen wiggled her toes up and down.

'I can't feel anything.'

'Let's have a look at the other one then.'

The sight of my red shirt and that of Thermal doing his dying swan act on my shoulder convinced her that Aileen was in no imminent danger of bleeding to death, so she came over and gave him a sympathetic pat on the head to make him feel better.

At least the prospect of a broken collar bone took his mind off his paw for a few moments and while his eyeballs were still revolving in their sockets I was able to slip an old ankle sock over his leg and fasten it with an elastic band.

'I'll just change my shirt and then I'll take him down to the vet's.'

Thermal is very good at being pathetic, it's one of the things he does best, and while he was in that sort of mood there was no need for the cat basket. I draped his blanket over the passenger seat and he curled himself into a ball and pretended he was at death's door.

For a cat Thermal travels rather well. It all started as a joke. He was fast asleep on the best cushion one day, and when Thermal sleeps he sleeps as though he's been drinking for a week. He was out cold and I was out of cigarettes. I put my head around Aileen's office door.

'I'm just popping down to Ali's for some cigarettes.'

She switched off her tape recorder and turned back to the computer.

'Well, do me a favour and take Thermal with you. I can't concentrate on anything with him snoring his head off.'

He does rather tend to snore in stereo, with both nostrils on full volume, so I picked him off his cushion and bore him out of the room as though I were serving him on a silver tray.

We went down the inside staircase, down the front steps, along the path, through the gate and out on to the pavement.

I tucked him under my left arm as I searched my pockets for the car keys, his legs dangling down back and front as though I'd hung him out to dry. I opened the passenger door and laid him on the seat and he was still snoring as I started up the car and drove away.

I pulled up outside Ali's, bought my cigarettes, turned the car round, drove home, climbed back up the stairs and plonked him down on his cushion and he had no idea that he'd even been as far as the hearthrug.

Aileen had been in the bathroom when we came back, washing her hands for want of a better expression, and she didn't really believe me when I told her that he'd never even opened one eye during the whole journey. So the next day I decided to prove my point.

We were going up to her mother's and it's a journey we make with some trepidation. Her mother is Irish and her father is a Yorkshireman. Her mother never shuts up and her father never utters a word except to say 'Oh aye' every half an hour or so.

I decided to take Thermal with us. He didn't take much finding. He was fast asleep in my desk drawer and perhaps I had better explain why.

Every afternoon, straight after lunch, I go back into the office and Thermal comes with me to give me moral support.

He finds that giving me moral support wears him out pretty quickly, so after a few minutes I open the deep drawer on the right hand side of the desk and he climbs in and has one of his famous long naps. I don't keep anything in the drawer except Thermal and an old typewriter cover so he can make himself cosy, and then as soon as he's settled down I shut the drawer.

I open it every now and then to ask him the odd question such as 'How do you spell squirrel?' or 'What is the meaning of life, Thermal?' He never answers, but it gives me a little thinking time and allows Aileen to shout out the answer from her office next door.

On this particular day Thermal had overslept and we were due at her mother's an hour ago, so I pulled out the drawer with Thermal in it and took it down to the car and stuck him on the back seat.

We drove to Lindley, calling for petrol on the way, and he almost drowned out the radio with his snoring. When we arrived I carried both the cat and the drawer into the house.

We had a cup of tea and a cupcake, then another cup of tea and a scone and still he slept like a kitten in front of the fire.

Aileen's father had already said two 'Oh aye's and so we must have been there for over an hour. Her mother had said all that she had to say and was just about to start all over again when Thermal awoke.

At first he gave one of his small stretches and then dropped off to sleep again, but very soon he was into one of his big stretches where every muscle of his body has to do a hundred press-ups and then run on the spot for three and a half minutes. It takes a little time but it's worth it.

He waited until they had all gone and done as they were told and then he gave one of his world-famous yawns and leapt out of the drawer, expecting a drop of some eighteen inches before he hit the ground. He hadn't allowed for the fact that, not only was his drawer now right on the other side of town from the desk, but it was also sitting flush on a foreign hearthrug.

He landed almost before he had taken off and jarred every little bone in his body. He just stood there, fur on end, staring first at Aileen's mum and then at Aileen's dad and thinking, 'What the hell am I doing here?'

I was sitting on the settee behind him and so I leaned forward and gave him a stroke to make him feel at home.

'Hello, Thermal.'

He jumped three feet in the air and tried to go straight up the chimney.

Since then we've been all over the place together. It's an easy-going relationship and the only awkward moment was when I refused to have his cat litter tray in the car. If I have to stop quickly I shall have quite enough on without being stoned to death.

He plays nodding head cats on the rear window ledge and specializes in frightening traffic wardens. I'm just waiting for the day when he asks if he can take driving lessons.

I shall say no. From there on it's only a short step to, 'Can I borrow the car tonight, Dad?' and I'm not having that. It takes me a good hour every night to catch him before I can put him to bed as it is – if he had the car I wouldn't have a cat in hell's chance.

I shall simply tell him that they won't let him drive because his paws won't reach the pedals and simply leave it at that.

But he wasn't thinking about driving today. He just lay on his blanket and licked his paw through the sock. He rather liked the sock, it added a touch of drama to the situation and he was all for a touch of drama. If he had his way we would have had a flashing blue light on the roof, together with a blaring siren to ease our way through the traffic. As it was he would have to make do with the sock, so he closed his eyes and tried to imagine that I was the flying doctor.

I wanted to try out a new vet. Not that I had any complaints about the old one who had previously looked after the cats, but I had watched over the past few months as the brand-new surgery had risen from the footings to the foundations to the splendid stone and glass edifice that now stood in the middle of its own private car park, with its nubile young trees and solid oak litter-bins.

I could see it now as I turned the corner. I had wanted to have a look inside for ages, but short of taking Arthur for a pregnancy test I had never had a reasonable excuse.

Large chrome letters spelled out the word *Surgery* over the entrance and I could almost smell the white hot technology champing at the bit as I carried Thermal across the tarmac, wrapped up tight in his blanket.

Here before me stood a monument to the new generation of veterinary science. There was bound to be a crash team, in green overalls with green rubber wellies and face masks, waiting to whisk Thermal into the operating theatre on a stainless-steel trolley. It might cost a bob or two more but it would be well worth it.

I pushed open the double doors with my forehead and stepped inside. The waiting room surpassed my wildest dreams. Done out in a white that hasn't even been invented yet, it gleamed with matching tiles and metal chairs that would have the most adventurous of germs signing on for income support.

This was the ultimate in the clinical approach. Not like the old vet where dog-eared posters of moth-eaten cats were plastered all over the walls, and adverts for worming powders embarrassed the hell out of the better bred animals who weren't used to that sort of thing.

All that was missing was any sign of human life. Maybe it was all done with robots. I couldn't find a bell to ring, so I sat down to wait. As if by magic, a nurse appeared at my elbow. Of course – close-circuit television, I should have known.

She wore a proper uniform, in whitest white, and her blond hair was tucked under a neat white cap. She had a small ladder in her tights but I suppose you are bound to get teething problems.

She stared hard at Thermal for a few moments and I began to wish I had given him a good scrub before I had brought him in. Then she stared at me and I wished I'd had a shower.

I said, 'It's my cat.'

She said, 'Is it?'

I said, 'Yes.'

She said, 'Oh.'

I said, 'His name's Thermal.'

She said, 'Is it?'

I said, 'He's cut his paw.'

She said, 'Has he?'

I said, 'Yes.'

She said, 'Oh dear.'

I said, 'He cut it once before.'

She said, 'Did he?'

I said, 'Yes – but it got better on its own.'

She said, 'Did it?'

I said, 'Yes – but this time I think it'll need stitching.'

She said, 'Do you?'

I said, 'Yes.'

She said, 'Oh dear.'

I said, 'This isn't a vet's, is it?'

She said, 'No – it's a dentist's.'

I said, 'I'll be off then.'

She said, 'Thank you for calling.'

I said, 'Don't mention it,' and I walked stiffly out into the empty car park, feeling her cold blue eyes on my back as a bitter November breeze ruffled the blanket under my arm.

Why do I do these things? Why don't I ever think things through?

I settled Thermal on the seat beside me and yet another pair of cold blue eyes settled themselves upon me.

'*I've never been so ashamed in all my life.*'

'I'm sorry – I never thought.'

'*You never do – that's your trouble.*'

'I know. You see, Thermal, what it is – I have the sort of mind that only pays me occasional visits. The rest of the time it sort of freelances, nipping off, doing exciting things on its own, leaving me to muddle through as best I can.'

'*You mean you're barmy.*'

'Well, yes and no. You see, I've carved myself a unique niche in this writing business. I must be the only man in this country who does more or less nothing at all and then writes about it.'

'*I suppose that can't be easy.*'

'No it's not. Other writers travel from pole to pole or right around the world in eighty days. I just spend my time doing things like taking the cat to the vet's.'

'*Or the dentist's.*'

I pulled the car to a halt at a zebra crossing and waited while an Indian couple traipsed across in single file. She wore a most elegant sari in red and gold and he was dressed to kill in a crisp white tunic.

The anoraks were a big mistake though. Anoraks don't go with the traditional Indian costume and it's about time somebody told them so. About time a designer came up with an alternative. A cape maybe. What were those nineteenth-century cloaks called that the women wore? They were fur-lined and would be just the job for this sort of weather. A pelisse, I think it was. I must look it up when I get home.

'*Have we arrived?*'

I jerked myself out of my reverie and slipped off the handbrake.

'No, not yet. I'm sorry. You see that's what I mean, I can't concentrate on any one thing for two minutes together. That's why I'm having all this trouble with my book and Jim Cochrane's expecting it any day now. God knows when he'll get it – this year, next year – '

'*Sometime, never.*'

'You could be right at that. I wish I was more like Aileen, she can shut out the entire world when she settles down to write, whereas I—' I broke off. A thought had struck me. 'You know, Thermal, that wouldn't make a bad title.'

'*Have we arrived?*'

'No. *Sometime, never.* I like it. I could work with that. It just about sums me up. Do you know, I can feel the confidence beginning to flood back already. That's probably been my trouble all along. You need the right title you see, otherwise you just drift aimlessly, not knowing where you're going. *Sometime, never* – yes, I like it. Thanks, Thermal. I feel like a new man. I am going to take this book by the scruff of the neck and I'm going to stick at it until it's finished.'

He shifted slightly in his blanket and examined the ankle sock which had now wrinkled itself down around his paw. He took a peek underneath and then looked up at me.

'*Do you mean – before or after I bleed to death?*'

CHAPTER SEVENTEEN

I can always tell when I am coming down with the flu. My skin goes all fragile and it's as though I've borrowed somebody else's testicles. I mentioned it to Aileen.

She was very sympathetic.

'Well, don't forget to give them back as soon as you've finished with them.'

I ran a hot bath. Doing this tells the germs that I know exactly what they are up to and that I'm not going to stand for it. They never take any notice but it's better than doing nothing.

I ran quite a lot of hot water before I decided to put the plug in to stop it all running out again. That's the trouble with flu, the brain shifts into a 'hands off' mode and takes on the role of a United Nations Observer. It sees everything but it does damn all about it.

While the bath was filling up I decided to make myself a hot lemon drink. I switched on the kettle and then thirty seconds later the plug flew out of the back because there hadn't been any water in it.

So I filtered a jug from the tap but forgot to pour it

into the kettle and the plug flew out again and this time the kettle rejected it and told it to push off until it had cooled down.

Then I *did* fill the kettle but forgot to switch it on and it was some twenty minutes or so later before I had actually boiled enough water to dissolve a sachet of Lemsip.

The bath was ready and waiting, but that first molten moment had gone and I like that bit – when you scream as you dip your toe in.

I lay back in the bath and topped it up with more hot water, feeling it swirl around my naked body.

'*I'll have a drink of my lemon now,*' I thought. '*Where is it?*'

I couldn't find it anywhere. I peered at the table I had set up by the side of the bath for my book and my cigarettes. No Lemsip.

'I must have left it in the kitchen,' I groaned, and brought my hand up from under the water to reach for the towel. Then I saw the mug. It was in my hand and had been under the water all the time.

Within twenty-four hours Aileen was lying in bed beside me, soaked in perspiration and complaining that her head was floating just beneath the ceiling.

We lay like that for two whole days. The phone rang and we let it. The doorbell rang and we pulled the duvet up over our heads. We drank a glass of water every now and then and I managed to stagger downstairs on only one occasion, to feed the cats.

I explained to them that they had given up Whiskas for Lent and that it was good for their souls. I don't think they believed me, but they were wonderful about it and took it in turns to sit on the end of the bed and worry about us.

It wasn't the first time I had been delirious with the flu – it always seems to take me like that – but I can't remember ever having had company before.

Aileen and I held long rambling conversations that

seemed terribly important to us at the time and I have a distinct memory of her sitting bolt upright in bed, eyes wide and staring. She turned and grabbed me by the skin around my nipples and shook me vigorously.

'Can you see me?'

I had some difficulty focussing properly. There was someone there, with damp hair and panic plastered all over her face. It could well have been Aileen.

'Am I here?' the voice insisted.

The fingernails dug in deep and the face pressed closer to mine. It *was* Aileen.

'Yes – I think so.'

She fell back on her pillow with a huge sigh of relief.

'Oh – thank God for that.'

Otherwise, the memory of those two days remains dim and distant, but eventually I was able to crawl out of bed and stay out of it for an hour or more.

I was so weak that it took me ages to open a tin of cat food, and then I had to have a lie down on the settee for a spell to recover.

Aileen was still in never-never land, however, and I had just flopped back into bed and dropped off to sleep once more when she woke me in another bout of sheer terror. This time her panic was such that both my nipples saw her coming and hid underneath my armpits.

'You've got to do something,' she shouted. 'They're demanding a blood sacrifice.'

I pushed her back on to her pillow and tucked the duvet around her.

'Don't worry, love – I'll sort it out.'

The next thing I remember was being downstairs, going from room to room, trying to find these people so that I could reason with them.

Then I thought, '*What am I doing?*'

I climbed back upstairs to where Aileen was sitting bolt upright in bed, waiting for Jack Nicholson and his axe to come splintering through the door any minute.

I tucked her up once more.

'It's all right, love,' I told her. 'They'd got the wrong house.'

'Oh thank you,' she cried. 'You're wonderful.'

'I know,' I said and climbed back in bed beside her.

The next day I was due to appear at a hotel in Heathrow to talk at a dinner and there was no way I was going to be able to make it, so I girded my loins and rang the organizer.

He wasn't the sympathetic type and I felt bad enough as it was – I had never let anyone down like this before.

'Whenever I feel the flu coming on,' he said, 'I just tell it that I'm not going to give in and it goes away – it's just mind over matter, that's all.'

I took a deep breath and blew right down the line. I don't suppose you can catch flu down the phone, but I hope you can. He could talk to it until he was blue in the face, but if it hadn't taken any notice of Aileen then it certainly wasn't going to take any notice of him.

By midweek we were both up and about, but if the spirit was willing then the flesh was absolutely knackered, and simply bending down to pick a milk bottle off the front step was a major operation.

'I'll go back for the other one in a minute.'

Aileen said she could feel the roots of her hair growing on the inside of her head and I knew exactly what she meant. My ears seemed to have put on a lot of weight and I was having difficulty keeping them properly balanced.

'How are we going to get to London on Friday?'

'On the train?'

'I suppose so.'

I would much rather take the car to London. I hate the traffic down there, but even more I hate the thought of lugging suitcases the length of King's Cross station.

While the engine itself comes to rest only a few hundred yards short of the taxi rank, the smokers' carriage at the far end of the train is still emerging from a dark tunnel just this side of Peterborough and it's one hell of a walk.

I love the convenience of the car. Aileen can pack all the clothes she might possibly need.

'What sort of a party do you think it will be?'

'I've no idea.'

'It might be a posh do.'

'It might.'

'On the other hand . . .'

With the car she can tip the entire contents of her wardrobe right into the boot and at a pinch we could strap her dressing table on to the roofrack. And we don't have to leave the party to catch a train just as the conversation is warming up and the gossip is beginning to fly.

I love having Aileen's company in the car. We sing raucous songs and make up very rude newspaper headlines from the letters of the licence plates on the cars in front. We can sink into long silences and yet still be very close to one another, or chatter non-stop all the way from junction 38 of the M1 right down to Hyde Park Corner.

Best of all I love inventing scenery for her. For a wife who can't see any further than the car window it is possible to transform the North Circular Road into the Lake District, or shorten the journey somewhat by pointing out all those delightful little antique shops that line the slow lane of the M25.

'There's one there with a thatched roof.'

'Sounds lovely – can we stop and have a look?'

'Not really – it's all yellow lines.'

She would mull this over for a mile or so and then a thought would struggle to the surface.

'They can't do much business.'

'How do you mean?'

'With all those yellow lines.'

I've been mulling it over as well, desperately preparing my defence.

'You have to come up behind them, on the B6259 out of Rickmansworth.'

'On the way back then?'

'Yes – if we have time.'

As long as my nerve holds out I can impress the pants off her.

'I didn't know you knew this part of the country so well.'

'Oh yes, love – like the back of my hand.'

I had a look at the back of my hand the other day. There are lots of little brown age spots coming through. I'd never noticed those before.

This time I only took the car as far as Wakefield. We do have the most wonderful railway station in Huddersfield. From the outside it looks the sort of place Queen Elizabeth the First might have stayed at on one of her journeys north. From the inside it looks like somewhere the Millwall supporters might have visited on their way back down south. But the line at Huddersfield runs from East to West and so we always drive over to Wakefield, where they have a direct Inter-City route to London, and the best British Rail staff I have ever come across.

They have held back the early morning train for us as we sprinted across the car park and parked the car for us when we didn't have the time to sprint. If only you could hear the public address system in the waiting room it would be just about perfect.

I slept for the best part of an hour and awoke to find that we had been joined at Doncaster by a rather elegant man, probably in his mid-fifties, who was thumbing through a leather-bound file and initialling various pieces of paper.

Usually I like to talk. I have met some lovely people on the London train. I once had Barrie Cryer all to myself for two and a half hours and he gave me a free crash-course on writing for comedians that turned out to be priceless.

And then there was a man called Harold who took me, step by step, through the daily routine of the average racing pigeon, with special emphasis on feeding and mucking out. You can't win 'em all.

But I didn't feel like talking today. My brain had now

225

curled up in a corner and hadn't even bothered to switch on the answering machine. So I stared into space and wondered how we were going to cope with the meeting that night.

The invitation had come from David Lascelles, the film producer, asking us to meet the cast of the forthcoming film.

'And we've got the perfect man to play you.'

'Not Jimmy Nail?'

'No.'

'Who then?'

'Jim Broadbent – have you seen any of his work?'

I was delighted. I had admired him for years in such programmes as *Only Fools and Horses*, and I had his wonderful spoof documentary, *A Sense of History*, on tape somewhere. I had had a look for it, but I couldn't find it anywhere.

To be honest I suppose I wasn't really the Jimmy Nail type – nor the Clint Eastwood type for that matter, although I hated to admit it.

Jim Broadbent was a much more vulnerable actor than either of them and I could identify with him. I just hoped that he could see something of himself in me.

I stared at my reflection in the train window and this moon-faced moron stared right back at me. What was he going to think of me? I bet he'd never played a Dalek before.

The man opposite seemed to have a problem. For some time he had been rubbing away at his left arm, just above the elbow. At first I thought it was just something he did when he was concentrating, but now he pushed his papers to one side and began to squeeze the muscle gently, as though he was expecting it to burst at any moment.

He was quite right to look worried. I would have been petrified. The muscle on his left arm was about twice the size of that on his right and it seemed to be growing as I watched. It was as though he had just started on a body-building course and was doing it one arm at a time.

He decided to investigate. He stood up and slipped off his jacket and I was able to see the thing more clearly. It was a lump about the size of an orange and it seemed to be moving – it was on its way round the back of his arm.

Every time he gave it a squeeze it sort of gave up and died on him. And then it would grow again, very slowly, as though someone were pumping air into it.

I wanted to wake Aileen. She ought to see this. But of course she wouldn't be able to, and I couldn't talk her through it with him sitting just across the table.

He undid a button at his wrist and then began to thread his right hand up the inside of his shirt sleeve until it was well past his elbow.

The lump must have seen him coming because it began to inch out of his way, right up his arm until it was sitting on his shoulder like a very small and very shy parrot.

He was getting desperate now and he obviously had no idea what on earth it was. And then the lump began to disappear down the back of his shirt.

I looked around me and found that I wasn't alone in my fascination. The foursome at the table across the aisle had stopped plotting the downfall of Norman Lamont for a moment and were sitting spellbound. A young woman on her way back from the toilet paused as she passed by.

The man wasn't aware of any of us. He decided he was on to a loser chasing it up his sleeve, so he tugged his shirt out of his trousers and went in after it round the back.

He hunched over, his forehead resting on his briefcase, and I half rose from my seat so that I could see over the top of his head.

It was on its way down past his shoulders and it paused for a moment, posing like Quasimodo's hump in the middle of his back. Granted it was only a very small hump, but if it had been on my back I would have been yelling for a nurse.

We held our breath as his hand travelled up the inside

of his shirt, and then he made a grab for it. The lump couldn't have been concentrating properly, either that or it had wrongly assumed that he wasn't the sort of man who would stoop to such a dirty trick.

He had it in his fist now and we all watched open-mouthed as he dragged it kicking and screaming out into the daylight.

It was a sock. A large grey sock. Not one of your fancy ankle jobs, but a great big woollen sock, the sort of sock you wear with stout shoes or wellingtons.

He stared at it for a moment or so, smoothing it out with his hand, and then he opened his briefcase and tossed it inside.

I could guess what had happened. If ever I am short of a sock when I pull the washing from the machine, the first place I look is up the sleeve of the nearest shirt. Aileen's briefs also have a habit of treating my shirts as a second home, a retreat from the hurly burly of the real world.

A long time ago, when the children were little, we had a washing machine that had been made by one of the heroes of our time, John Bloom. A Rolls Rapide I think it was, and we thought it was wonderful.

It did, however, suffer from the odd bout of indigestion and once chewed up a whole bunch of soft toys that we had popped in with the rest of the washing.

It looked like the aftermath of the Alamo when we pulled them out. There were limbs everywhere, and although we rushed them straight into surgery, most of the menagerie were destined to spend the rest of their days as amputees.

The next morning, as I walked into the office, I could feel something digging into my hip. Must be my car keys, I thought, so I slipped them into another pocket.

I was turning the memory over in my mind as I hauled our suitcases the entire length of King's Cross station. I think we were just passing through Watford when one of our fellow travellers caught up with us.

'You have to hand it to that bloke with the sock, don't you?' he said. 'He never batted an eyelid, did he?'

'No.' I agreed. 'Certainly took it in his stride.'

But I couldn't help wondering just how calm he would have been if, like me, he'd gone to the toilet during his mid-morning break and pulled a teddy bear's arm out through the zip in his trousers.

There was a car waiting for us. Or to be more precise, there was a man holding a board with my name written on it waiting for us. He had parked the car round the corner.

As we waited for him to bring it over I couldn't help thinking of my early days with the BBC.

They paid me twenty pounds a time for writing and recording my short stories. It would have been a fair rate of pay if the train fare to London and back hadn't completely wiped it out.

I never complained, never asked for any expenses – they might not have asked me again if I had, and you never know, it could lead to bigger and better things. And I suppose eventually it did – it just took twenty-five years longer than I hoped it would.

After nervously recording my very first piece I emerged from the bowels of Broadcasting House with just enough loose change in my pocket to buy myself a cup of coffee on the train home, but not enough for the tube fare to King's Cross station. So I walked all the way. It took me hours and I was soaked to the skin.

And now, when I could easily afford the taxi fare, they had sent a car for us. Sometimes I think life comes at us the wrong way round.

I must admit, however – I do rather enjoy being spoiled. As I sat that night in one of the most wonderfully surreal houses in London, with antique bicycles hanging from the ceiling, surrounded by an enormous collection of ancient cameras and art-deco juke boxes of all shapes and sizes, I felt the adrenalin begin to flow once more and with it came just a glimmer of the confidence that had deserted me these past few weeks.

Perhaps my life wasn't so ordinary after all. Our host Richard Loncraine, the film's director, had spent all day cooking a splendid Moroccan meal that had managed to ease our taste buds out of temporary retirement.

Over there on the settee with Richard's wife Felice, Aileen sat deep in conversation with Sian Thomas, who was to play her in the film. Their two heads were close together and their hair was almost interchangeable – Sian was working on the rest.

Julie Walters was just as I hoped she would be. I had fallen in love with her many moons ago and she didn't disappoint me now. As we talked I would no sooner catch a glimpse of an educated Rita then in would come Mrs Overall to bring the conversation back down to earth.

Jim Broadbent and I were taken on a tour of the house. Down to the basement via a series of iron staircases, past walls built of glass bricks and then back up flight after flight of stairs to a bedroom where a huge motorized rickshaw from the Far East waited patiently at the foot of the bed.

Eventually we reached a bathroom on the top floor where stood an enormous bath with a sort of pagoda at the tap end, incorporating a huge brass shower-head.

'It was originally used to calm down lunatics.'

We thought about that for a moment and shuddered.

'Richard got it from a mad house.'

Jim nodded.

'Well, it'll certainly feel at home here, won't it?'

There was something missing, however. Where were all those towering, overblown egos that are supposed to be so rife in the film business?

Certainly there weren't any in evidence tonight. What we had here was a bunch of real artists who were professionals down to their fingertips. Any writer would be glad to hand his work over to them, safe in the knowledge that they would polish it and add to it something of their own.

As I sat back and sipped my whisky a self-satisfied smirk greased its way across my face. If I hadn't written the books in the first place then none of this would be happening.

I took another sip of the whisky and as I did so I spotted an ego doing the rounds over by the fireplace. It was only a very small ego but it looked ever so pleased with itself.

So there was one here after all and I wondered who it belonged to. It caught my eye and hurried over to have a word with me. I recognized it now. It was mine.

Around lunchtime the next day another car arrived to whisk us back to the station, and as we passed through London's crowded streets I practised my queenly wave, just the slightest movement of the forearm together with an almost imperceptible break in the wrist. The practice would come in handy for the world première.

The train journey passed in no time at all and before we knew it we were standing on Wakefield station once again.

I was slightly miffed not to find a troop of native bearers waiting to carry my luggage over to the car. But never mind, the time would come.

I helped Aileen into the passenger seat and then dropped the suitcases into the boot. A heavy drizzle had replaced the pale sunshine of London and it looked as though it had settled in for the day. It was certainly several degrees colder up here and the light was fading fast. I wished I had brought an overcoat with me. Never mind, be home soon.

I turned the key in the ignition and nothing happened. I turned it again and then again but the car had no idea I had even got back from London.

'Come on.'

It was either the starter motor or lumbago, probably both. I slipped the handbrake off, and then, as the drizzle began to take itself more seriously, I began to push the car out towards the main road.

My ego didn't know what to make of it. It was a very young, and highly impressionable ego and at first it just sat there and shivered in the driving rain. It just couldn't believe that this soaking specimen could be that successful author who had picked it up in London.

Then, after it had watched me struggle all the way across the car park, it waited until I had joined the long queue lined up at the traffic lights before deciding to make a break for it.

As the lights changed to green and I put my shoulder to the door frame once more, with a blessed incline just around the corner, it suddenly bolted off towards the railway station and the next train back to London.

I suppose it was for the best really. Yorkshire is no place for an ego. This is where egos get strangled at birth.

That evening I rang Nick to tell him of our adventures in the big city.

'You haven't borrowed any videos, have you? The one with Jim Broadbent in *A Sense Of History?*'

'No, not me.'

'I can't find it anywhere and I wanted to have a look at him in action again.'

'Well, he's on that Victoria Wood tape as well, in a spoof documentary – a day in the life of someone or other.'

'Oh, right. Thank you. I'll have a look for it.'

Just before I went to bed that night I found the video and pressed the fast-forward button until I saw Jim striding out past a row of terraced houses. I switched up the volume.

'Well, I think I thought – why me? – sort of thing. I'm not really Charlton Heston material, apart from one of my thumbs being double jointed. I'm really a fairly ordinary man.'

He paused at a door and went in, and as he did the title of the sketch came up over the picture. *A Fairly Ordinary Man*, it said.

He would probably play me rather well. It seemed he'd had more than enough practice.

CHAPTER EIGHTEEN

Aileen took the silk shirt from the wardrobe and slipped it over her shoulders.

'You've got it on inside out.'

She let it slide down her bare back, at the same time holding on to the cuffs, and I watched admiringly as it miraculously turned itself the right way round. She slipped it on again and began to fasten the buttons, which I couldn't help thinking was a bit of a shame, and then I noticed that she was also wearing that look of hers, the one that tries to be very firm and doesn't quite make it.

'Are you listening to me?'

'Yes of course.'

'Good.'

The shirt was one of my favourites. It's see-through in a certain sort of light and we certainly had that sort of light in the bedroom. I'm just lucky, I guess.

'This is the last time this year.'

'Absolutely.'

'We must have the books away by the thirty-first.'

'We will.'

'So we won't accept any more invitations until they're finished?'

'Not a single one. After tonight it's nothing but work.'

'Good.'

She popped the final button through the final hole and, out of sheer habit, turned to face herself in the mirror.

'What does that look like?'

'It's cockeyed. You missed the bottom buttonhole.'

'Damn it.'

She sat down on the edge of the bed and began to undo them all.

'We shall be late.'

I adjusted the cushion on the cane chair and made myself comfortable.

'Don't worry, love – you just take your time.'

We drove out on to the moors, to one of those old stone villages where the cobblestones smell of freshly-baked Hovis and every other house seems to have a pub all to itself.

They are nice people. He runs a small computer business and she runs him. She also has a very light touch when it comes to making pastry and she is the proud possessor of a PhD in Yorkshire puddings. But just as I was looking forward to a second pot of Colombian coffee and a good long chat around the dining table, he pushed back his chair and stood up.

'Why don't we pop out for a drink?'

He had a sideboard over there bulging with the stuff, and apart from that a regular army of hailstones had been rattling the dachshund-flap in the kitchen door all the way through the treacle tart and custard.

'I'm quite happy to stay here.'

'Come on, a bit of fresh air will do us good.'

As we stepped out of the porch and into the freezing cold the dachschund looked at us as though we must be mad. Mind you, he is a supercilious little devil and I never did have much time for him. When they first moved into the country they said they hoped he wouldn't worry the sheep. And I don't suppose he ever has, unless the sheep worry that they might fall over him in the dark.

At least we wouldn't have far to walk. Inn signs swung drunkenly down the main street as far as the eye could see and the most promising one of all hung over the pavement right across the road from us. He yanked open the garage door and I pointed towards the golden glow in the pub window.

'What about that one?'

'There's no atmosphere over there,' he said, and we all piled into his car and drove off towards God knows where.

We had a bit of a chat in the car, or as much of a chat as you can have when you are peering round two four-foot high headrests.

Not only couldn't we hear what the driver and his passenger in the front seats were saying to us – we couldn't see them either. Every now and then I would lean forward to try and take in the odd word and at the same time gratefully catch sight of a brown brogue hovering over the clutch pedal, a length of stockinged thigh in the passenger seat and a painted fingernail tapping gently on a menthol cigarette. It was comforting to know they hadn't got out and left us to it.

We seemed to have been driving for ages. In fact we had been in the car for some twenty minutes and I was just thinking that it couldn't be much further when he nipped down a slip-road and on to the M62.

A very pleasant MFI lorry hoped that we would have a nice day and a rather sullen pantechnicon glowered at us and told us to keep our distance.

'Not be far now,' he shouted over his left shoulder.

I leaned forward and spoke in a loud, clear voice.

'You did say we were going for a drink, didn't you?'

'Twice,' he said. 'Once during my national service in Hong Kong and then again in Cyprus.'

236

I can't be doing with these headrests, they take over the whole damn car.

'How much further is it?' I shouted.

'August,' he said. 'First two weeks in August – but not every year.'

Eventually we pulled into a large car park the size of Doncaster and then trudged through the driving rain towards an enormous black and white pub.

'I think you'll find it well worth the trip,' he told us. But I doubted it the moment we stepped through the doors to be met by the massed tonsils of the Royal West Yorkshire's Twittering Yuppies.

Above the bar was a large board bearing an honours list of real ales. Ales sounding something like:

'Tolpuddle's Old Geriatric'
'Throxton's Vastly Superior'
'Clogginton's Old Abominable'
'Cleckheaton's Mostly Peculiar'

It went on and on. 'Right. What are you having?' he asked, pointing to the board.

'I'll have a gin and tonic,' said Aileen, and everyone within earshot went deathly quiet.

'Oh no you won't,' he said. 'Not in here.'

'Oh yes I will,' insisted Aileen and she did. You don't muck about with Aileen – not if you have any sense.

Unfortunately I am not made of the same stuff and I finished up with half a pint of 'Thropley's Ghastly Diarrhoea' in my hand, or something that sounded very much like that.

'Two of those and you pass out,' he told me. I couldn't help thinking that it was a long way to drive in order to render oneself unconscious.

The couple at the next table ordered a ploughman's lunch, at a quarter to nine in the evening, and were served with two cute triangles of buttered brown bread and a small cube of Stilton, sitting up pompously on a single leaf of purple lettuce.

'Do you get many ploughmen in here?' I asked the landlord, but he wouldn't have recognized a touch of sarcasm if it had jumped up and bitten him. It was a pity. I don't go in for the barbed remark very often and it spoils it when they fail to hit the target.

'Not much farming round here now,' he told me. 'Pretty well died out, it has.'

From starvation I shouldn't wonder.

But the most depressing thing about the pub was the effect it had on the customers. Our friend is an intelligent man who can hold an intelligent conversation, but for the next two hours all he could talk about was 'Real Ale'.

We had two lovely women with us whom we could chat up and seduce. I knew for a fact that one of them was wearing a see-through silk shirt, and yet all he wanted to talk about was the beer.

It was just the same at other tables. All around the pub the customers would take a sip and then close their eyes with such reverence that it might have been communion wine they were drinking. It had certainly been blessed by the landlord, who must have been making a bomb out of this place.

Our friend slept like a baby all the way home while his wife drove and I pointed out to Aileen all the pretty houses and the quaint little shops clustered on the hard shoulder of the M62. I only had a pint myself. I had tried something that sounded vaguely like 'Risley's Instant Disablement' as my second half and my eyeballs were revolving.

It had been a total waste of time. The evening, like the beer, had gone rather flat. Aileen had been right, we would have been far better off working at home.

Perhaps I could still fit in a couple of hours. I glanced at my watch as I switched on the hall light. Midnight. Yes – a couple of hours at least.

I helped Aileen off with her coat and then with her

jacket. She turned towards me and a couple of seconds later the silk shirt came rippling round all on its own, in the way that silk shirts always do.

'Are you coming to bed or are you going to work for a while?'

She smiled up at me, a sleepy sort of smile, and I quickly reconsidered my position.

I suppose I could always make an early start in the morning instead.

One by one the children rang in to see what we were doing for Christmas.

'We shall have to cancel it this year,' I told Aileen. 'We shall have to work right through.'

At least it solved one problem for them, the sort of headache that always crops up at this time of the year.

'*Are we going to go to your mother's for Christmas or are we going to mine?*'

'*It's up to you — but you know what she's like.*'

It was a pity. I enjoy their company at Christmas. I always have, and when they were small there was the added excitement of Santa Claus and those huge pillow cases dangling from the bedposts.

That slice of our life came to an abrupt end when they decided to give Santa's grotto a miss and elected instead to join the queue outside the Chesterfield Co-operative Society's do-it-yourself department, so they could shake paws with the famous Dulux sheepdog. Christmas was never quite the same after that.

I switched on the Amstrad and as I sat there, waiting for it to clear its throat, I remembered those days of Christmas past.

Year after year we would trot down to the Presentation Convent to watch the Nativity play. Nick would have spent months polishing his acting techniques until he eventually became perhaps the finest third shepherd ever to be seen in that august establishment.

By the time his final year at primary school came

around he had risen like a rocket through the ranks and had firmly established himself as a fully-fledged second shepherd. They talk of his performance still – wherever and whenever old shepherds gather together.

As a Protestant in a Catholic primary school he had little chance of playing the part of Joseph. Maybe I should have mentioned to the headmistress that he had at least half a pint of Jewish blood coursing through his veins? Perhaps that might have swung it in his favour.

Perhaps not. It would have meant him having to learn lines and he was never very keen on that. Shepherds just have to stand around in a group and mutter and he was extraordinarily good at standing around, and even better at muttering. Stick to what you know is what I say.

Sally never took part in the Nativity play. As a ballet dancer of some promise she was always hired as the warm-up act – a sort of seven-year-old Salome in a leotard with lots of stiff netting tacked around her bottom.

The Amstrad gave a grudging grunt to let me know that it was now ready for me, so I plucked a small white kitten from the keyboard and flexed my fingers in readiness.

I once wrote a piece on the Nativity for *Woman's Hour* and I wondered if I could use it again. I didn't see why not. If you can't have a flashback at Christmas – when can you have a flashback? So I pulled open the filing cabinet and began fishing around, and after a fruitless search under the letter 'N' I found it kicking its heels under the letter 'C' for Christmas.

For a man who can never remember where he left his cigarette packet three minutes ago I have a remarkable facility for being able to produce anything I have written over the past twenty years at the drop of a hat.

Every single piece is filed under an appropriate letter. Articles on my mother are stashed away in strict date order under the letter 'M', and everything I have ever written about the cats can be found curled up in a ball and fast asleep under 'C'.

I must be one of the few people this side of Glasgow

to have found a good use for the divider marked 'Mc'. That's where I file all the little stories about my mother and her cat.

Perhaps I should file my cigarette packet under the letter 'C' and then I might be able to lay my hands on it when I want it. No, best not – the cats have quite enough bad habits without me turning them on to twenty cigarettes a day.

The three sheets of yellowing paper crumbled to a fine dust as I held them in my hands. Well no, perhaps that is going over the top just a little, but the corners were decidedly dog-eared and the paper did have a rather jaundiced look about it.

I remembered writing this piece. The full stop on my typewriter was sticking at the time, the comma had a crush on it and they used to go everywhere together, and so I had to flick the key with my forefinger and thumb at the end of every sentence. I had perched on the edge of the bath that night with the typewriter sitting up on the ironing board, and I typed and flicked away until the early hours so that I could record it and send it down the wire before breakfast later that morning. How unlike the home life of our own dear Jeffrey Archer.

I smoothed the top sheet of paper with my hand and began to read.

WOMAN'S HOUR – DECEMBER 1978

Have you ever wondered what Jesus looked like? Was he tall and bearded or was he black and clean-shaven? Did he really look like Robert Powell or have the artists been getting it wrong all these years?

Well, perhaps I can help, because you see – I've seen him . . .

Three flicks at the end of that last line. My fingernail must have been black and blue by the time I'd finished. But then we writers are supposed to suffer for our art and as I read on it proved to have been well worth the effort.

I could remember the day as though it were yesterday.

There must have been a hundred of us proud parents huddled together in that cold hall, squatting on those long low forms that had been designed to accommodate the tiny bottoms of five-year-olds.

Every now and then we would hear a shriek of agony from some six-foot father as the cramp struck home and then a hush settled over the audience as the lights began to dim and a huge gold cardboard star, suspended on a wire, began its journey from the back of the hall towards the stage.

Halfway along its path it dithered slightly and then shuddered to a grinding halt.

A teacher, who had spent the last half hour leaning against the wall bars, strode purposefully forward, brandishing one of those long poles with a hook on the end, the sort they use for opening and shutting fanlights.

She arrived so promptly and so well equipped that obviously she must have done this at least half a dozen times during rehearsals.

She stood on the end of one of the forms and, swinging the pole around her head, she cracked the star with such force that it belted off down the wire, towards the stage, at about thirty miles an hour.

It slammed against the curtains and the audience sat fascinated as it spun like a Catherine wheel. Eventually it slowed down and stopped and that was the signal for the entry of the three wise men.

They were dressed in white flannel sheets and their average age was somewhere around seven years and three months — you had to be a mature student to be a wise man in those days.

They wore little white towels on their heads secured by those narrow striped belts with the 'S'-shaped buckles. The towels had been supplied by the landlord of the local pub and were the ones he draped over the pumps at closing time, with the result that each wise man had the words

'McEwan's Export' emblazoned across his forehead.

The wise man in the middle was the one with the gold. I could tell because he had a large brown paper parcel under his arm with the word 'GOLD' written on it.

I think the wise man on the left was the one with the frankincense and he was carrying it in what looked suspiciously like a Fairy Liquid bottle.

The wise man with the myrrh was very shy. He had his back to us and was sobbing gently.

The curtains parted and the scene before us was that of a stable. Centre stage we could see Mary sitting on a long form – very like those that were giving the audience so much trouble out in the hall.

We could also see a donkey with huge ears, a lamb represented by a five-year-old under a bedside rug, and a cow with the most pornographic set of udders I have ever seen on the British stage.

The producer, Mrs Micklewight, had opted for participation rather than historical accuracy, with the result that the stable was a trifle overcrowded. There must have been seventy kids in there.

The children in the dressing gowns were the citizens of Bethlehem and the small boy in the chef's hat must have been the innkeeper.

The others had been told to use their imagination and come as assorted animals. About nine of them had their right arms shoved up emus, teddy bears abounded, there was a four-foot duck, and a huge black and white panda with wicked green eyes was threatening to take over the show.

In the meantime, the shy wise man with the myrrh had decided against a theatrical career and was sitting on his mother's knee in the front row.

The children had written their own script, and the high spot of the afternoon was the arrival home from work of Joseph, looking very much like a refugee from *Fiddler On The Roof*.

He paused at the door, not for dramatic effect, just to avoid standing on his beard. He approached his wife.

'Hello, Mary, what's going off? It's a bit crowded in here.'

Mary smiled sweetly.

'Hey up, Joseph. Have you had a good day at work?'

'Not so bad, Mary. What's going off?'

'It's me, Joseph. I've just seen an angel.'

'Have you really, Mary? And what was it the angel had to say to you then?'

'He said I were having a baby.'

'Did he really, Mary – when?'

'Now, Joseph.'

Mary bent herself almost double. Then, bunching her fists and screwing up her face in agony, she gave the most God Almighty grunt.

'MMMmmmmmmmmmmmmmmmmmmmmm.'

Opening her eyes, she pointed triumphantly over towards a crib just left of centre stage.

'There it is.'

Joseph seemed slightly taken aback by Mary's virtuoso performance and had to be prompted from the wings, but he quickly pulled himself together and then wandered slowly over towards the crib. Mary could hardly contain herself.

'What sort is it, Joseph?'

Joseph wandered slowly back.

'I've just had a look, Mary, and I think it's a little lad.'

'Oh, Joseph. I've always wanted a little lad. What shall we call him?'

Joseph thought about that for a while, long enough to be prompted by a small voice from underneath the bedside rug. Joseph glowered at the unwanted intrusion and then carried on.

'Well, I had thought of calling him Walter after me dad, Mary, but to tell you the truth I've always had a soft spot for the name Jesus meself.'

Mary smiled. A sweet, motherly smile.

'Right then. That's what we'll call him.'

And with that she leaned over and shouted in the general direction of the crib.

'Nah then, Jesus!'

And a little toddler, who all this time had been hidden, curled up in the crib, jumped up and shouted back.

'Hey up, Mam!'

I shall never forget that afternoon and the sight of Jesus, Joseph and Mary taking a final curtain call, flanked on either side by a duck, a panda and a bedside rug. It brought the house down.

I flicked through the fading pages and read the final paragraph.

And so if you want to know what Jesus looked like, then I am just the man to tell you about him. He isn't tall and bearded and he doesn't look a bit like Robert Powell.

He's about two foot tall – definitely clean-shaven. He's as black as coal, he's got a lovely smile and he speaks with a Derbyshire accent.

We worked solidly all through the first half of December, but even though Christmas wasn't going to happen for us, there were still some seasonal jobs to be done.

I had decided that this year I was going to organize the Christmas cards properly – I couldn't afford a last minute panic. If I did six a day from the seventeenth of November right through until the seventeenth of December I could wipe off the list and still leave a few days spare to deal with any unexpected arrivals. That way I would be able to add a little message in each card and do the job properly.

By the fifteenth of December I calculated that I could still make it if I averaged ninety cards a day for the next two days, but by the eighteenth my plans were all in tatters and I had ten boxes, each containing twenty cards, stacked up on one end of the long table while I sat in the middle and worried about them.

Aileen put her head round the door and peered straight through me.

'Are you in here?'

'Yes.'

'What are you doing?'

'The Christmas cards.'

The list is laid out in alphabetical order and I made a start on the first entry. She came over and stood behind me.

'I wish I could help you.'

'Don't worry about it.'

'I feel so helpless.'

I signed the card with a flourish, licked the envelope and placed it on the table to my right. That was better, I was under way now and I had the makings of a pile on which I could build.

'Shall I do the stamps?'

'Yes, if you like.'

She patted the enormous mound of boxes to my left.

'What are these?'

'Those are what I have to do.'

She pulled up a chair and sat down beside me, patting the card I had just finished.

'And what is this?'

'That's what I've done.'

'Oh dear.'

I handed her the stamps and she began tearing them into foot-long strips, bringing her organizational skills into play.

'Do we have a system?'

'Yes – I'm working alphabetically.'

'So who is this one for?'

I glanced at my list.

'Aileen Armitage.'

'That's me.'

'That's right.'

'Oh goody.'

She ripped open the envelope and held the card up to the light.

'Oh it's lovely.'

'You've got it upside down.'

'I'll go and have a look at it properly, under my close-circuit television.'

'You do that.'

She trotted off back to her office and I screwed up the remains of the tattered envelope. My embryo pile had disappeared – just like that.

I put a tick by the side of her name and noticed that she hadn't even sent me a card at all last year. If I didn't get one from her this year I would have to cross her off my list.

Day after day we locked ourselves away, working at our desks, and Bridie crept around the house, trying to make herself invisible.

'Bridie – come and have a coffee with us.'

'No. You two will be wanting to put your heads together and be having a think.'

She gave in eventually and stood there, leaning against the fireplace, cradling a mug of coffee in her hands.

'For goodness sake, Bridie, come and sit down.'

'I'm all right here. I'm taller standing up, like a dog is sitting down.'

I thought about that for a few moments. I could use it if only I could understand it.

I peered out of the window and saw Alfred in the park, waiting for Mrs Bramley to stop talking and catch up with him. Knowing Mrs Bramley he might have to wait there all day. He gave a great big sigh and plonked his bottom down on the path. He knew it as well.

Then I noticed something about him that I had never noticed before. He was taller sitting down than he was standing up. Isn't life wonderful?

Aileen really had the bit between her teeth now. Her story had taken hold of her and begun to pull away like a thoroughbred racehorse. Mine just sat there like Alfred and wagged its tail at me every now and then, but gradually the pages began to pile up and I began to glow with that lovely feeling of having given birth.

Granted my manuscript looked somewhat anorexic by the side of Aileen's bouncing baby, but that didn't matter – it was my flesh and blood and I would love it dearly and see to it that it had a good education and ate lots of fresh vegetables.

We took time out to buy presents for family and friends, and Aileen decided that, even if Christmas was going to pass us by this year, we must have a tree in the hall.

'It wouldn't be the same without.'

We would also have to buy some glass baubles. Thermal had taken to eating them straight off the tree last year and become a dab hand at knocking them down off the lower branches.

I would hear him crunching from miles away, but by the time I arrived on the scene he would be spitting out the metal pin and enjoying a deeply satisfying burp.

'We could get some in Sheffield.'

I had a book signing to do over there, at Dillon's in the Meadowhall shopping complex, and it was going quite well until an announcement came booming over the loudspeakers.

'Santa Claus and Bugs Bunny have now arrived in the Oasis Centre.'

Within seconds the shop had emptied and I was left all on my own with a great pile of books and a disappointed pen. I might have been able to cope with Santa Claus, but bringing in a heavyweight like Bugs Bunny as his sidekick meant that I didn't stand a chance.

At least it gave us time to shop around for the decorations, and eventually we found ourselves in a department store which proved to be a veritable Aladdin's cave.

'But just look at the prices.'

I am very good at spending money, I have a natural flair for it, but the thought of paying so much just to add a little roughage to Thermal's quite adequate diet seemed rather ridiculous. The young assistant tended to agree with me.

'Terrible price, aren't they?'

'It does seem a bit much.'

She peered cautiously over her shoulder to make sure we weren't being watched, and then whispered in my ear.

'You want to try my Uncle Eddie's stall in the market. He's got unbreakable balls.'

Aileen, who, due to her lack of sight, quickly becomes disorientated in a crowded shop, perked up noticeably at this exciting news and I left the decision up to her.

'What do you want to do, love?'

'Let's go over to the market. I wouldn't miss Eddie's unbreakable balls for the world.'

I called in at the chemist's on the way home and had to wait my turn while a busy throng of customers sorted themselves out into an orderly queue. The young woman in front of me plonked a small baby on the counter and stared at her shopping list.

'A packet of Tampax Super, please.'

'Sorry, love – we've sold out.'

'What do you mean, you've sold out?'

'Christmas rush.'

I couldn't help thinking what strange presents people seem to be buying one another these days. Or maybe I had got it all wrong. Perhaps they were painting them in bright colours and hanging them on their Christmas trees – they would look quite pretty. I closed my eyes and tried to imagine the look on Thermal's face as he knocked one down and started chewing.

Chris Holt came bouncing out from his dispensary and stopped dead in his tracks as he spotted an old man who was systematically pushing his way to the front of the queue.

'What on earth are you doing here, Tom? The pubs are still open.'

The old man's face told a story all of its own as he shook his head in sorrow and disgust.

'I can't be doing with pubs at Christmas – they're full of bloody amateurs.'

An elderly woman leaned over my shoulder and whispered in my ear.

'I do wish they'd hurry up, don't you?'

I let her have my place. I could have stayed there all day.

We worked hard, right up to Christmas Eve, and without Bridie to entertain us the house took on an unnatural quiet, which was broken only by a loud crunching noise that floated up the stairs from the hall.

Thermal had taken on Frink as an apprentice and was showing her the tricks of the trade. Eddie's unbreakable balls were going the way of all flesh. It was unchewable balls that I had really wanted. I think I shall try the chemist's next year.

It was exactly six o'clock that afternoon when Aileen let out a great cry of triumph and came running in to see me.

'I've finished!'

We did a little dance around Arthur on the Chinese rug. It's a tradition in our family and dates back to six o'clock that afternoon.

After a celebratory cup of tea she tucked herself up on the settee with her tape recorder and I sat down at her word processor and began to read aloud the first of the five hundred and six pages of *The Jericho Years*.

It was four o'clock on Christmas morning by the time I had finished. My voice had cracked up twice on the way there, but it managed to hold out through the compelling twists and turns, and rallied strongly to come back on song for the dramatic climax.

'That was terrific.'

'Do you really think so?'
'I know so.'
'Oh good.'

After a year in the writing we had almost forgotten what had happened in those earlier chapters and it had been as though we were reading the book for the very first time. It worked well, and for the past ten hours we had been caught up in the turbulent lives of the characters Aileen had created.

I suddenly felt terribly tired and went back into my office to switch off my computer for the day. It sat there on my desk, wondering where the hell I'd been all its life, and I sat down in my chair and stared blankly at its glowing face.

The last words I had written stared back at me:

The cornflake took no notice. Poor little sod – it was probably a very young cornflake, still wet behind the ears, and had no idea that this was merely part two of a well-rehearsed manoeuvre that Thermal has perfected over the years.

I pushed my chair back and thought about what I was doing with my life. There was Aileen in the very next room, bringing to her pages all the power and the passion of her own private world.

And here was I – writing about the adventures of a very young cornflake, about to be mugged by a small white cat who can talk in italics. Was this a proper job for a grown man, I asked myself?

If there had happened to be a grown man in the room at that moment I might very well have asked him, but I looked round and there was only me.

And then I had a brilliant idea. I could slip in an extra line, something about Thermal being a cereal killer. I hugged myself with pleasure at the thought and then tucked my chair in closer to the desk.

What the hell. I enjoy writing about cornflakes and kittens and dogs who wear berets – they are a few of my favourite things.

'It's time we were tucked up in bed,' Aileen called as she drifted past my door.

'Shan't be a minute,' I shouted back. 'I just want to make a note of something.'

With only six days to go there was no way I would finish the book this year — next year would have to be soon enough.

At that moment I couldn't have cared less. This was the most wonderful way to earn a living and I would be happy if it never came to an end.

In fact, sometime never would do very nicely indeed.